SILENCING THE

LONE ASSASSIN

SILENCING THE LONE ASSASSIN

by John A. Canal

PARAGON HOUSE
St. Paul, Minnesota

First Edition, 2000

Published in the United States by
Paragon House
2700 University Avenue West
St. Paul, MN 55114

Manufactured in the United States of America.

Library of Congress Cataloging-in-Publishing data

Canal, John A., 1945-
    Silencing the lone assassin / by John A. Canal.– lst ed.
        p. cm.
    Includes bibliographical references and index.
    ISBN 1-55778-782-4
        1. Kennedy, John F. (John Fitzgerald), 1917-1963 –Assassination.
    2. Oswald, Lee Harvey. I. Title.

E842.9 C359 2000
364.15'24'092–dc21
                                                                    99-045392

10 9 8 7 6 5 4 3 2 1

For current information about all releases from Paragon House,
visit the web site at http://www.paragonhouse.com

JOHN FITZGERALD KENNEDY
35th President of the United States
May 29, 1917–November 22, 1963

Credits

My sincere gratitude is extended to the following for permission to reprint photographs and other graphic material.

CONTENTS

List of Figures

Preface

The assassination of John F. Kennedy has received more attention and analysis perhaps than any other single event, much less murder, in American history. While officially, according to the Warren Commission, Lee Harvey Oswald alone assassinated JFK, other investigators, researchers, and authors have pointed fingers at the CIA, FBI, Mafia, anti-Castro Cuban exiles, pro-Castro Cubans, military industrial complex, ultra-right-wing activists, and yes, even President Johnson! In fact, if every shooter from even half of all the conspiracy books were actually present in Dealey Plaza when JFK's motorcade passed through, there would have been more lead flying around than at Gettysburg! Kennedy's limo would have had more bullet holes than Bonnie and Clyde's Ford[1] when deputies gunned them down. Some authors are grossly in error, purposely distorting the truth or simply lying in their endeavor for the "quick buck!" In one of the books I read on the subject the author stated that he personally interviewed the "confessed assassin" of JFK. He further stated that he had to travel to Europe to do this because that's where the "assassin" was hiding out. Others even falsify documents or photos. For example, I can't believe how well Mary Ann Moorman's Polaroid photo of the "grassy knoll," taken when the motorcade passed, has been so stunningly "enhanced" over the years. When first examined it was difficult to distinguish what the fuzzy images behind the picket fence (to the front and right of the motorcade) actually were, although conspiracy theorists insisted one was someone shooting at JFK. A recent so-called "enhancement"[2] clearly shows a man in uniform, who has come to be known as "Badgeman," shooting towards the president. In a few years, with more "enhancements" (can I call them "doctored photos?")

we'll be able to read "Badgeman's" police unit designation imprinted on his badge. More than a dozen witnesses, by the way, who had a good view of that area, testified that they never saw anyone behind the picket fence.[3] In addition, the ballistic, scientific, and medical evidence proved beyond a reasonable doubt that the two bullets that struck President Kennedy came from behind him.[4]

Misinformation and deception on the subject run rampant, largely fueled by the fact that conspiracy "story lines" tend to be more arousing, sensational, and appealing to the reader. Nonetheless, my intent in writing this book is to record what I believe to be true. I am confident that I have presented (in Part I) a convincing case to show that, while there is no doubt that a number of groups disagreed with or hated JFK, and "rogue" elements thereof may have even seriously considered his assassination, *Lee Harvey Oswald, alone, assassinated President John F. Kennedy!*

Additionally, I will present (in Part II) further evidence to show that Jack Ruby was hired by the Mafia to "silence" Lee Harvey Oswald for what he knew and what the Mafia was afraid he'd tell authorities.

I am honored to tell you how I came to my conclusions.

PART I

LEE, THE LONE ASSASSIN

Figure 2: Dealey Plaza

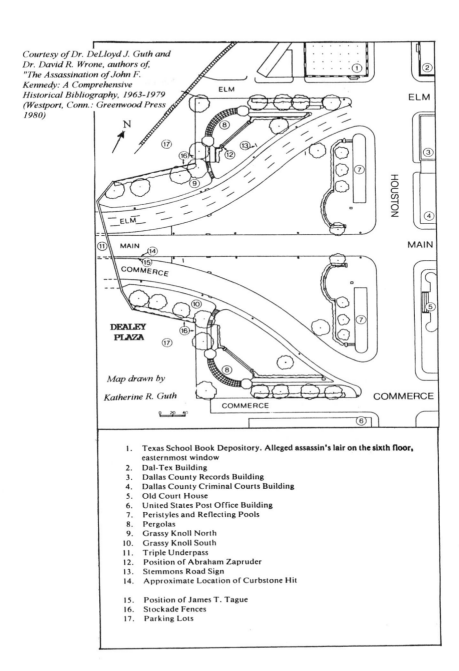

Courtesy of Dr. DeLloyd J. Guth and Dr. David R. Wrone, authors of, "The Assassination of John F. Kennedy: A Comprehensive Historical Bibliography, 1963-1979 (Westport, Conn.: Greenwood Press 1980)

N

ELM

ELM

HOUSTON

MAIN

MAIN

COMMERCE

DEALEY PLAZA

Map drawn by

Katherine R. Guth

COMMERCE

COMMERCE

1. Texas School Book Depository. Alleged assassin's lair on the sixth floor, easternmost window
2. Dal-Tex Building
3. Dallas County Records Building
4. Dallas County Criminal Courts Building
5. Old Court House
6. United States Post Office Building
7. Peristyles and Reflecting Pools
8. Pergolas
9. Grassy Knoll North
10. Grassy Knoll South
11. Triple Underpass
12. Position of Abraham Zapruder
13. Stemmons Road Sign
14. Approximate Location of Curbstone Hit

15. Position of James T. Tague
16. Stockade Fences
17. Parking Lots

3

Commission Exhibit No. 697

Figure 4: Photograph of presidential limousine taken during motorcade

CHAPTER 1

The Gunman or Gunmen?

In Dallas, on November 22, 1963, at 12:30 P.M., as the motorcade of President John F. Kennedy passed in front of the Texas School Book Depository, perhaps the most unforgettable gunfire of our time emphatically punctuated the sounds of cheering spectators, and critically wounded both the president and Texas governor, John Connally. At approximately 1:38 P.M., while the governor was desperately struggling to survive his wounds, the world was stunned by the announcement that President Kennedy was dead.

At 1:50 P.M., Lee Harvey Oswald, a Communist sympathizer, who would soon become a suspect in the assassination, was arrested and later charged with the murder of Dallas Police Officer, J. D. Tippit. But, by early the next morning, Oswald, was also charged with one of the the greatest crimes of the century, the assassination of President John F. Kennedy.

Incredibly, still another murder would highlight the first weekend of this American nightmare. Just as if choreographed for Hollywood, on Sunday, November 24, at 11:21 A.M., in the basement of Dallas police headquarters and right in front of dozens of law enforcement personnel, Oswald himself was shot by a local nightclub owner Jack Rubenstein. Less than two hours later Oswald was declared dead.

Within a week President Lyndon Johnson appointed a seven-member commission, headed by Chief Justice Earl Warren to investigate the assassination. The "Warren Commission," as it predictably had been named, released its report to the public on September 27, 1964. The commission concluded that Lee Harvey

Oswald, acting alone and using his WWII-vintage bolt-action rifle, fired three shots from the southeast corner window on the sixth floor of the depository. They said one shot "missed." Another, they reported, hit JFK in the upper back, exited his throat, and then struck Governor Connally (sitting in front of the president) in the right shoulder, exiting just below his right nipple.[1] Amazingly, they claimed, that same bullet, after exiting below the governor's nipple, passed through his right wrist, and finally lodged just under his skin in his left thigh. If you weren't counting, that was *seven* wounds from *one* bullet! The commission further concluded that Oswald's third shot caused JFK's fatal head wound. While conspiracy theorists vehemently attacked most aspects of the commission's account, three conclusions seemed to draw most of their fire.

The "Magic Bullet"

Critics said the commission's contention that one bullet could have caused the seven wounds to JFK and Governor Connally was preposterous![2] For one thing, they said, the nearly "pristine" condition of the bullet, mysteriously found on a stretcher at Parkland Hospital, was far too good for it to have caused all those wounds.[3] In addition, they went on, the seven wounds didn't even "line up!"[4] Moreover, the critics clamored, the only possible explanation for the apparent delay, estimated to be from one-half to one and one-half seconds (as viewed on the Zapruder film*) between the reactions of the president and the governor to their wounds was that they were hit by different rounds! It's easy to see why these skeptics sarcastically named that bullet the "Magic Bullet." While their sarcasm may have been annoying, their assertion that the seven wounds must have been caused by *two* bullets had critical implications. This was because the Zapruder film showed that JFK and Governor Connally received those seven wounds within a time frame that was so short (even with the "delay") it

---

*Abraham Zapruder was standing on a pedestal at the westernmost section of the pergola at the time of the shooting and took the most famous film of the assassination.

would have been practically impossible for *one* gunman with a bolt-action rifle to fire *twice*. Based on that, the critics believed they had "breakthrough" proof of a conspiracy. [2 bullets within (not more than) about one and one-half sec. = 2 gunmen = conspiracy].

"Head Back"

Conspiracy theorists also pointed out that when JFK received his fatal head wound, his head "rocked back," not "forward," indicating that he was shot from the front. They received support on that point from numerous "ear witnesses" who said they heard shots coming from the "grassy knoll," which was ahead and to the right of JFK's limo when the shots were fired. In addition, their claims were reinforced by Dr. Cyril Wecht, a leading forensic pathologist, who has maintained to this day that JFK's fatal head wound was caused by a shot from the front. Then, because the president's back wound showed inarguably that a shot came from the rear, the strong indications that a second gunman fired a shot from the front seemed to leave little doubt that there was a conspiracy.

One Gunman, Three Shots?

Another major aspect of the commission's lone assassin theory was unacceptable to the critics. They argued that, even if there were three total shots as the commission claimed,* it was impractical to even consider that one gunman could fire three times (twice with accuracy) in such a short time (early estimates were that all three shots were fired in about six seconds). Again the implication was clear. There had to be more than one gunman! (2 gunmen = conspiracy).

---

*Most critics still maintained the seven wounds to JFK and Governor Connally were caused by "two" almost simultaneous shots, not "one" shot (bullet)! Therefore if one missed, and counting the president's head wound, that would have been four total.

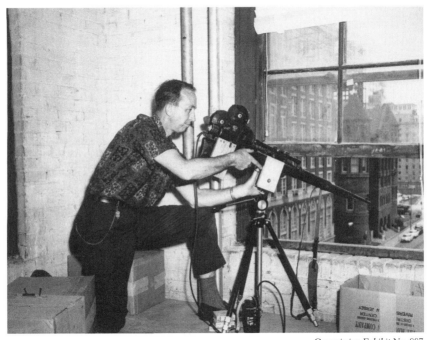

Figure 5: Photograph taken during reenactment showing C 2766 rifle with camera mounted

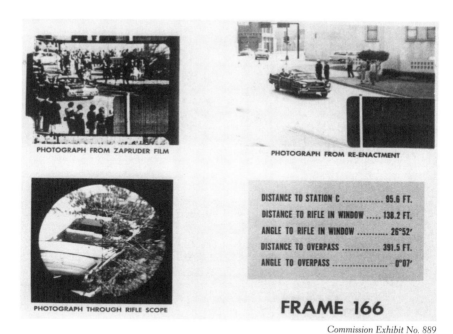

Figure 6: The first shot has just been fired

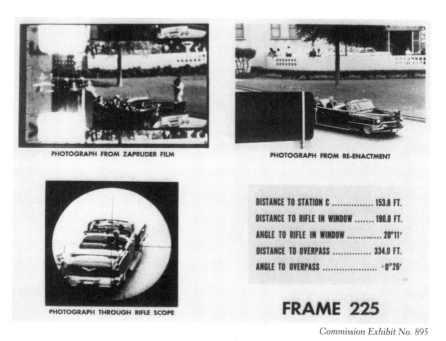

Figure 7: The second shot has just been fired

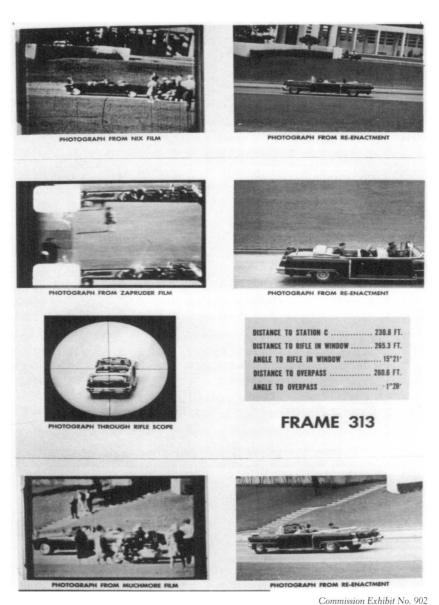

PHOTOGRAPH FROM NIX FILM

PHOTOGRAPH FROM RE-ENACTMENT

PHOTOGRAPH FROM ZAPRUDER FILM

PHOTOGRAPH FROM RE-ENACTMENT

PHOTOGRAPH THROUGH RIFLE SCOPE

DISTANCE TO STATION C .... 230.8 FT.

DISTANCE TO RIFLE IN WINDOW .... 265.3 FT.

ANGLE TO RIFLE IN WINDOW .... 15°21'

DISTANCE TO OVERPASS .... 260.6 FT.

ANGLE TO OVERPASS .... 1°28'

FRAME 313

PHOTOGRAPH FROM MUCHMORE FILM

PHOTOGRAPH FROM RE-ENACTMENT

Commission Exhibit No. 902

Figure 8: The third shot is fired

At this point, based just on the Warren Commission's apparently "weak" account of the number of shooters and shots, the critics seemed to have an airtight case that at least two gunmen were in Dealey Plaza on November 22, 1963, as part of a conspiracy to assassinate JFK.

The Tables Turn

Over the course of more than three-and-one-half decades since the assassination, the arguments of the conspiracy theorists that seemed so compelling early on have steadily become dubious. On the other hand, the findings of the Warren Commission, at least on what seem to be the most critical issues, have been re-peatedly supported. For example, the Clark Panel in 1968, the Rockefeller Commission in 1975, and the House Select Com-mittee on Assassinations (HSCA) in 1979 all reported, "in con-cert" with the Warren Commission, that "President Kennedy's wounds were caused by two bullets, shot from the rear!"[5]

The HSCA findings were especially credible in that they had employed nine of the foremost forensic medical experts in the country with extensive experience in gunshot wounds. These ex-perts were granted unrestricted access to all the autopsy x-rays, photographs, and reports, and given the funding needed to use the latest scientific equipment to conduct their tests.[6]

"Even More Support"

In 1992 an article published in the *Journal of the American Medi-cal Association (JAMA)* provided additional support for the War-ren Commission's report on the number of gunmen and shots. In that article the accounts of Dr. "J" Thornton Boswell and Dr. James Joseph Humes, the two former navy pathologists who performed (Humes was actually in charge) the autopsy on JFK the night of November 22, 1963 at Bethesda Naval Medical Center in Mary-land, were published "publicly" for the first time. Both stated for JAMA that "President Kennedy was struck by only two bullets that came from above and behind…!" [please see Appendix IV].

The "Not So Magic Bullet"

"Pristine" Condition

The critics argued that the "pristine" condition of the Magic Bullet, supposedly found on a stretcher at Parkland Hospital, was too good to have caused the seven wounds to JFK and the governor, as the Warren Commission claimed, and must have been "planted." The commission's claims on this issue, however, received the support of two highly touted experts.

Larry Sturdivan, an army scientist at the Aberdeen Proving Grounds, explained that the Magic Bullet, even after causing seven wounds, was not "deformed" significantly because it had lost velocity when it passed through JFK without hitting any bone.[7]

Lone assassin killed JFK, AMA interview results say

Associated Press *5-20-92*

NEW YORK — Two doctors who tried to revive the mortally wounded President Kennedy and two others who performed the autopsy are certain he was shot twice from behind by a lone gunman, as the Warren Commission concluded.

Dr. George Lundberg, editor of the *Journal of the American Medical Association*, said Tuesday the four doctors dispelled conspiracy theories about the 1963 assassination in rare interviews for its May 27 issue.

The doctors maintain Kennedy was shot twice from behind by a single gunman, as the much-disputed commission report decided in 1964, Lundberg told reporters at a news conference. The governmental inquiry determined Kennedy was killed by Lee Harvey Oswald.

Many of those who support conspiracy theories about the assassination think Kennedy was shot from the front and that the government tried to cover up what really happened by moving the

autopsy to a Navy hospital.

Lundberg said the journal, as a professional publication devoted to scientific research, has "a very good chance, perhaps the best chance, of setting to rest the talk of conspiracy around the autopsy.

"I think the non-availability of information has contributed greatly to people wondering," he added. "We're trying to put an end to the wonderment."

Pathologists James Joseph Humes and Thornton Boswell, who conducted the autopsy at Bethesda Naval Hospital in Maryland, told the journal that bullets always leave a small hole where they enter and a beveled crater where they exit.

"We proved at the autopsy table that President Kennedy was struck from above and behind by the fatal shot," Humes said. "The pattern of the entrance and exit wounds in the skull proves it. This is a law of physics and it's foolproof."

Associated Press

Figure 9: Please see Appendix IV for entire *JAMA* article

Dr. Michael Baden, chief forensic pathologist for the HSCA, in regard to the Magic Bullet, stated, "I've seen similar bullets that have inflicted gunshot wounds. The bullet was traveling slow enough that, while its speed and density were still greater than the bone it was hitting, it was not moving so fast as to deform seriously the metal jacket." [8]

Another charge by the critics regarding the condition of the Magic Bullet (CE-399) hasn't been referred to as often as some of the others, but still deserves to be addressed here. In essence, the charge is that "the weight of the lead, missing," which was approximately 2.6 grains [437.5 grains = 1.0 oz.], "from CE-399, was less than the total weight of the six fragments that were either removed from, or left undisturbed in, Governor Connally." The conspiratorial implications were of course that another round [by another shooter] must have caused some of the governor's wounds. This charge is aptly answered by Gerald Posner in his *Case Closed.* Posner states, "*Some question whether less than three grains of lead was enough metal to make the six fragments in Governor Connally. Dr. John Lattimer squeezed an equivalent amount of the lead core from a 6.5 mm bullet and was able to create forty-one fragments the size that Dr. Gregory described.*" [Dr. Gregory is the surgeon who removed the bullet fragments from Governor Connally's wrist].

The Seven Wounds "Line Up"

In the summer of 1964 the FBI and Secret Service, using stand-ins, survey equipment, and a camera mounted to a telescopic sight, conducted trajectory tests for the Warren Commission that concluded a single round fired from the southeast corner window on the sixth floor of the book depository ("sniper's nest") could have caused the back and throat wounds to the president and the wounds to Governor Connally. [9]

In 1978 the Warren Commission's conclusions regarding the Magic Bullet's trajectory were confirmed by the results of tests performed by experts for the HSCA. Using mock-ups of JFK and Governor Connally, two separate trajectory lines were established, one based on the president's back (entrance) and throat (exit) wounds and the other on his throat wound and the governor's back (entrance) wound. Both lines pointed towards the "sniper's nest."[10]

In 1992 the commission received even more support for its Magic Bullet theory. That's when, as part of an episode of *Frontline*, Failure Analysis Associates (FAA) used computer modeling and impressive animated graphics to show how one bullet could have caused the seven wounds to JFK and Governor Connally [please see Appendix V].

At this point it should be noted that the first of Governor Connally's five wounds (shoulder) was "elongated." This means the bullet entered at an extreme angle, perhaps nearly "vertical," which also means it was "tumbling." Based on the fact that bullets don't "tumble" unless they hit something, and the only thing between Governor Connally and the "sniper's nest" at that moment was the president, the bullet must have hit JFK before Governor Connally! The bottom line is then, that Governor Connally's "elongated" shoulder wound very much supports the theory that one bullet caused the back and throat wounds to JFK and the five wounds to Governor Connally.[11]

Only a few months ago former President Gerald Ford, who served on the Warren Commission, publicly admitted that he "altered" the commission's statement describing the location of the entrance wound to JFK's upper back. Even though Ford swore that his "adjustments" were a "small change and intended to clarify meaning," critics were quick to say that this was just more proof of a government cover-up of an assassination conspiracy. The main concern of this author, though, was whether or not FAA had used the statement that Ford changed as a basis for their tests. I was able to ascertain from Dr. Angela Meyer, FAA's director of marketing, who participated in their analysis of the assassination, that only authenticated photographs were used as a basis for their calculations. Therefore the results of Failure Analysis Associates' computer modeling tests showing that one bullet (the Magic Bullet) could have caused all seven wounds to JFK and Governor Connally, in spite of Gerald Ford's revelation, stand firm!

The "Delay?"

One element of the Magic Bullet theory that the Warren Com-

mission had some difficulty explaining, and the HSCA supporting, was the apparent "delay" between the reaction of the president and the governor to the same shot. That delay was estimated
to be anywhere from one-half to one and one-half seconds in du-
ration. For all practical purposes, the HSCA agreed with the
commission's "weak" explanation that, based on previously documented instances, such delays were actually "not-so-unusual"
among gunshot victims. In fact, the committee noted that in many
cases the victims didn't even realize until much later that they'd
been shot.[12]

Ironically, since then, enhancements of the Zapruder film have
shown that all the controversy over the "delay" between the reactions of JFK and Governor Connally to the same bullet has been
academic. Indeed, the enhanced footage clearly shows the president and the governor reacting to being wounded at the same
instant.[13] The president can still be seen waving to the crowd up
until frame 226 when his arm began to rise and his elbow suddenly jerked off the limo (frame 227).[14] Simultaneously the
governor's posture and facial expression changed abruptly, certainly as a reaction to his wounds.[15]

If any questions remained over the "delay" between the reaction of JFK and the governor to the same bullet, FAA's meticulous analysis of an enhanced copy of the Zapruder film answered
them once and for all. They observed that, during frames 223-
224,* when the president received his back and throat wounds,
the right front of the governor's suit lapel "flipped up" from his
chest in the exact location where the suit and his shirt have a
bullet hole from the round that exited below his right nipple.[16]
The fact that most critics avoid mentioning this important evidence in itself indicates its weight in support of the commission's
Magic Bullet theory.

_____

*As Gerald Posner explained (in much greater detail) in *Case Closed*, the time
JFK was hit can be pinpointed quite accurately by subtracting his reaction
time (estimated to be between one-tenth to two-tenths of a second or 1.8-3.66
frames) from when his arm began to rise (frame 226) and his elbow jerked off
the limo (frame 227).

Ballistic and Scientific Evidence Support
the Magic Bullet Theory

Besides Failure Analysis' sophisticated computer modeling tests, the "elongated" entrance wound to Governor Connally's shoulder, the enhancement of the Zapruder film plainly showing that the president and the governor were wounded at the exact same time, and the testimony of Sturdivan and Dr. Baden regarding the Magic Bullet's condition, two other extremely significant facts help prove beyond any reasonable doubt that one bullet caused the seven wounds to JFK and Governor Connally.

Fact 1. Robert Frazier, an FBI firearms identification expert, and Joseph Nicol, superintendent of the bureau of criminal identification and investigation for the state of Illinois, independently

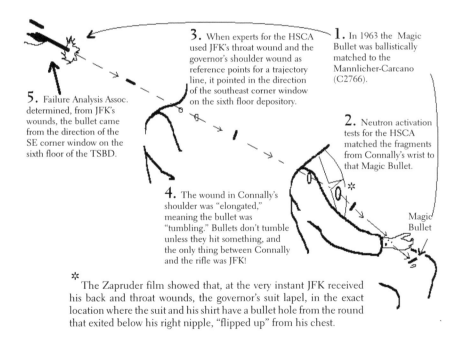

3. When experts for the HSCA used JFK's throat wound and the governor's shoulder wound as reference points for a trajectory line, it pointed in the direction of the southeast corner window on the sixth floor depository.

1. In 1963 the Magic Bullet was ballistically matched to the Mannlicher-Carcano (C2766).

5. Failure Analysis Assoc. determined, from JFK's wounds, the bullet came from the direction of the SE corner window on the sixth floor of the TSBD.

2. Neutron activation tests for the HSCA matched the fragments from Connally's wrist to that Magic Bullet.

4. The wound in Connally's shoulder was "elongated," meaning the bullet was "tumbling." Bullets don't tumble unless they hit something, and the only thing between Connally and the rifle was JFK!

Magic Bullet

* The Zapruder film showed that, at the very instant JFK received his back and throat wounds, the governor's suit lapel, in the exact location where the suit and his shirt have a bullet hole from the round that exited below his right nipple, "flipped up" from his chest.

Figure 10: Linking the Magic Bullet to JFK's back and throat wounds, Governor Connally's five wounds, and the Mannlicher-Carcano (C 2766)

conducted tests that matched the Magic Bullet to the sniper's Mannlicher-Carcano.[17]

Fact 2. Dr. Vincent Guinn, a highly regarded expert in neutron activation, conclusively matched the Magic Bullet to fragments taken from Governor Connally's wrist.[18]

A Shot from the Rear Caused His Head Wound!

Supporting Medical, Ballistic, and Scientific Evidence

The Warren Commission's medical findings alone seemed more than convincing that JFK's head wound was caused by a shot from the rear. The testimony of Dr. James Humes, the naval pathologist in charge of the autopsy, was powerful. He stated, *"After the brain was removed, we looked more closely at the wound [head], and noted that the inside of the rear of the skull bone was absolutely intact and beveled and that there could be no question from whence cometh that bullet—from the rear to the front!"*[19] Doctors Thornton Boswell and Pierre Finck, who assisted Dr. Humes, both validated his conclusions,[20] as did pathologists for the Clark Panel, the Rockefeller Commission, and the HSCA. Buttressing those compelling if not inarguable findings was ballistic and scientific evidence that *matched* the bullet fragments recovered from the brain of the president to the Mannlicher-Carcano found on the sixth floor of the depository to the rear of where the president was when he was shot!*[21]

---

* In 1977, Dr. Vincent Guinn, a nuclear chemist from the University of California at Irvine, using "neutron activation" testing, concluded that the Magic Bullet (CE-399), the fragments removed from Governor Connally's wrist (CE-842), the fragments recovered from JFK's brain (CE-843), and the fragments found on the rear floor (CE 840) and on the front seat (CE-567) of the limousine, altogether represented only two bullets.[22] More specifically, he determined that CE-399 (the "Magic Bullet") and CE-842 (the fragments recovered from the Governor's wrist), each having an antimony content of approximately 800 parts per million, were both part of the same bullet.[23] He further determined that CE-567 (the 44.6 grain "nose" fragment found on the front seat of the limo), CE-840 (the fragments found on the rear floor of the limo), and CE-843 (the fragments recovered from the president's brain), each having an antimony content of approximately 600 parts per million, were all part of a second

Nonetheless, die-hard conspiracy critics stubbornly maintained that only a shot from the front could cause JFK's head to "rock back."

His Head Jerked Forward and Then Rocked Back!

These critics were finally taken aback, however, when Itek Optical Systems, in a CBS documentary, showed by computer enhancement of the Zapruder film that JFK'S HEAD ACTUALLY "JERKED" FORWARD 2.3 INCHES (consistent with being shot from the "rear") BEFORE IT ROCKED BACK! The forward movement was so subtle that it had been undetectable before Itek's analysis.[26]

---

bullet.[24] *Portions of both bullets (CE-399 from one bullet and CE-567 from the other) had been previously matched, independently, by Robert Frazier and Joseph Nicol, ballistics experts for the Warren Commission, exclusively to the Mannlicher-Carcano (C 2766).*[25]

At this point, while trying not to disrupt the flow of the presentation of the evidence and information herein, I feel compelled to point out what I believe are misstatements in the HSCA report regarding the bullet fragments recovered from JFK's brain and those found in the limousine. In the paragraph on "neutron activation analysis" on page 45, it is written, "…it was highly likely…that one of the two fragments recovered from the floor of the limousine and the fragments recovered from the President's brain…were from a second bullet." This statement is incorrect in two ways.

First, four fragments were recovered from the floor of the limo, not two.

Second and much more important, the phrase, "highly likely" should never have been used by the committee in its report to describe the "degree of certainty" of Guinn's conclusions. While Guinn himself characterized that "degree of certainty" in his report as being "highly probable," he stated later in his testimony that the brain fragments "VERY CLEARLY" matched CE-567. Unfortunately however, when the HSCA described the degree of certainty of Guinn's conclusions in their report, they inexplicably chose to use their own much less definitive phrase "highly likely." In doing so they left the door wide open for critics to say that Guinn's tests were inconclusive when they were actually anything but.

Most important, though, the committee's statement is incomplete. It reported that the brain and one of the floor fragments "were from a second bullet," but, incredibly, failed to even mention CE-567 (a 44.6 grain "nose" fragment found on the front seat of the limo) which Guinn's tests proved was also part of that "second bullet." Their omission was extremely significant because ballistics experts had previously matched CE-567 to the Mannlicher-Carcano (C 2766) found on the sixth floor of the depository. This means that if the

It should be mentioned that Dr. Guinn's conclusions, as well as the results of a "spectrographic" test, performed on November 23, 1963, and neutron activation analysis performed in 1964 by the FBI, on assassination bullet fragments and specimens, have been the target of a hail-storm of criticism from conspiracy theorists (please see Appendix VI for more information about the FBI's

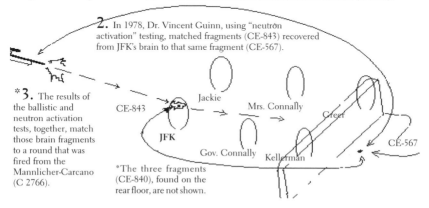

1. In 1964, Robert Frazier and Joseph Nicol, ballistics experts, independently matched CE-567, a 44.6 grain "nose" fragment found on the front seat of the limo, to the Mannlicher-Carcano (C 2766).

2. In 1978, Dr. Vincent Guinn, using "neutron activation" testing, matched fragments (CE-843) recovered from JFK's brain to that same fragment (CE-567).

***3.** The results of the ballistic and neutron activation tests, together, match those brain fragments to a round that was fired from the Mannlicher-Carcano (C 2766).

Jackie

CE-843

Mrs. Connally

Greer

JFK

Gov. Connally   Kellerman

CE-567

*The three fragments (CE-840), found on the rear floor, are not shown.

Note: This author believes CE-567, after exiting the president's head, impacted and dented the chrome windshield frame, before dropping onto the front seat. He also believes CE-569, a 21.0 grain "base" fragment (not shown), also found in the front of the limo, after exiting JFK's head, impacted and cracked the windshield before hitting the dash and falling to the floor in front of the front seat. While neutron activation tests showed that CE-840, CE-843, and CE-567 were all part of the same round, logically, CE-569 (not suitable for that type of testing) was also part of that round. CE-569 was ballistically matched to the Carcano.

Figure 11:
Matching the brain fragments to the Mannlicher-Carcano (C 2766)

committee had properly reported the match between the brain fragments and CE-567, the critical link between those brain fragments and the Carcano would have been clearly established.

It is my belief that this lack of complete and accurate reporting by the HSCA has caused even praiseworthy authors such as Gerald Posner to make statements in their work that could be more meaningful. For example, Posner wrote on page 342 of his outstanding book *Case Closed*, "…the fragments from Kennedy's brain matched the three testable fragments found on the floorboard of the limousine…." Again, it's far more important to state that the brain fragments matched CE-567, which was found on the front seat (not on the floor) and ballistically matched to C 2766, so that a clear connection can be made between the brain fragments and that same rifle.

spectrographic test and an important validation of both the FBI's and Dr. Guinn's neutron activation analyses).

The "Jet Effect"

Getting back to the main discussion about JFK's head rocking back, Dr. Luis Alvarez, a Nobel Prize-winning physicist concluded, based on extensive laboratory tests, that JFK's head rocked back even though he was shot from the rear as a result of a scientific phenomenon called the "jet effect." In this case the jet effect occurred when bone fragments and brain and tissue matter burst out of JFK's head towards the front, causing a "thrust" which violently rocked his head "back."[27]

Alvarez' conclusions received support from John K. Lattimer, a World War II combat surgeon and ballistics expert, in his 1980 book *Kennedy and Lincoln: Medical & Ballistic Comparisons of Their Assassinations*, Lattimer had conducted 12 physical experiments in which mock-ups of human heads were struck from behind by a 6.5 mm bullet. In each instance the "jet effect" caused the specimens to rock back towards the shooter.[28]

The "Blood Cloud"

Just recently, in a documentry on the History Channel, *Case Closed* author Gerald Posner pointed out that, if the Zapruder film is stopped at the instant the president received his head wound, a "cloud of blood" is clearly visible *"in front"* of his head, final proof that the fatal missile came from the rear.

One Gunman, Three Shots... It Can Be Done

The third major aspect of the Warren Commission's "one gunman" theory that the critics find unacceptable is the contention that one person could have fired all three shots (two accurately) in what was first estimated to be only about six seconds. Over the years the commission's conclusions on this issue have also been reinforced.

A CBS Test Supports the Warren Commission

In 1975 the Warren Commission's claim that one gunman could have fired all three shots received support from a CBS documentary. In that documentary, 11 volunteer marksmen each tried firing three shots with the Mannlicher-Carcano as fast and with as much accuracy as they could. The average time taken for the three shots was 5.6 seconds, with the target hit two out of three times.[29]

HSCA Gunmen Use the Carcano's Open Sights

In addition, in 1977, reconstruction tests for the HSCA showed that, using the open iron sights vs. the scope, it was possible to fire two shots in only 1.66 seconds (three shots in 3.33 seconds) and still hit the target.[30] The results of those tests made the assassin's "feat" of firing three shots (two with accuracy) in such a short time seem much less difficult to accomplish.

The Firing Took Over Eight Seconds, Not Six

More recently in his book *Case Closed*, Gerald Posner presented a highly compelling if not indisputable argument that the first* shot was fired at about frame 160 on the Zapruder film. This finding was of critical importance because it meant the total time between the first shot and the third (frame 313), at .0546 sec./frame, was actually over eight seconds (vs. about six, the earlier estimate), making the Warren Commission's claim that one gunman could have fired all three shots much more believable. Posner

---

*Because, at that point, no one in the limo showed any sign of being hit, it was evident the first shot was a miss. Posner believes the first bullet, deflected by an elm tree branch that protruded into the assassin's line of fire, caromed off the pavement and struck a curb 520 feet from the depository, causing a concrete chip to strike an onlooker, James Tague, in the face. The facts support Posner's theory. Virgie Rachley, a depository employee, testified, "I saw a shot or something hit the pavement...you could see the sparks..." She was certain she saw the sparks before the second shot.[33] The FBI, from spectrographic tests, concluded that the curb had in fact been struck by a bullet.[34] Moreover, a large elm tree in front of the depository is along a straight line from the sniper's nest in the depository to the curb that was struck.[35]

based his conclusion on facts and testimony that included the following:

1. Governor Connally testified that, just after the president's limousine made the turn onto Elm Street, he turned to his right because he heard a noise which he "immediately took to be a rifle shot."[31] The Zapruder film in fact clearly shows the governor turned to his right at about frame 162.[32]

2. In 1979, Brown University student David Lui observed, while studying a copy of the Zapruder film, that "a young girl, running to keep pace with the presidential limousine, stopped abruptly and turned toward the Texas School Book Depository...."[36] Indeed, the film shows that she started turning toward the depository at about frame 160.[37] The young girl, Rosemary Willis, told Lui that she stopped when she heard a shot![38]

3. New enhancements of the Zapruder film reveal that just after Rosemary Willis started turning toward the depository, the president suddenly stopped waving. A moment later, after first looking to his right and then left toward Mrs. Kennedy, he resumed waving. At that point, Jackie looked back in the general direction of the book depository.[39] Logically, she heard the first shot, just as her husband had, but obviously [and tragically] neither of them recognized it as such.

In some ways it seems as if some divine power had evidently called upon a simple elm tree branch in order to give a great man a warning shot, and one last chance to live. It is absolutely gut-wrenching for me to think that, after that first shot, no one near JFK yelled "Get down!" A historic opportunity...missed!

A Very Crude Test

In spite of all the support the Warren Commission has received on this issue, it still seemed incredible to me that one person could fire three shots with a bolt-action rifle (two with accuracy) in just over eight seconds. I decided to try a crude experiment (actually very crude) using a video I had recorded on the assassination that included the Zapruder footage. I started the video just as the Zapruder film showed the motorcade passing the book depository and "pretended to be aiming a rifle." I squeezed the trigger of my "imaginary rifle" just an instant before the little girl stopped running (first shot fired). Then, with the video still playing, I "closed my eyes" and pretended to eject the shell casing (bolt up and back), chamber a new round (bolt forward and down), take a brief moment to aim through "my scope," and squeeze the trigger a second time. A split second later, I opened my eyes to see President Kennedy bringing his clenched fists up to his throat. Eerily, I had squeezed "my trigger" at just about the same instant as JFK and Governor Connally were hit. I quickly "closed my eyes," repeated the reloading and aiming sequence, and squeezed the trigger for the third time. Just as I did, I opened my eyes to see the president's head being blown apart. I was stunned! I had squeezed "my trigger" precisely when JFK received his head wound.

Despite the crudeness of my experiment, I was now convinced beyond any doubt that one gunman could have fired three shots (two with accuracy) within eight seconds.

In Conclusion

The abundance of medical, ballistic, scientific, visual, and other evidence referred to in this chapter strongly reinforces the Warren Commission's "one-gunman" theory. The point, though, that deserves special emphasis is that *every "testable" bullet fragment recovered from JFK's brain, Governor Connally's wrist, and the limo, as well as the Magic Bullet, was matched to only ONE rifle, the Mannlicher-Carcano found on the sixth floor of the Texas School Book Depository (TSBD).*[40]

Recalling the findings of Failure Analysis Associates mentioned earlier in this chapter, it's important to add that they used "reverse computer projections" from the wounds of the president and governor to point to where the bullets came from. As you might have guessed, those projections centered on the southeast corner window on the sixth floor of the TSBD.[41]

The term "gunman" has been used repeatedly thus far. In chapter 2, that "gunman" will indeed receive an identity!

CHAPTER 2

Meet Lee Harvey Oswald

The material in chapter 1, compiled from an extensive number of sources, strongly upholds the Warren Commission's account that one gunman, from the direction of the southeast corner window on the sixth floor of the Texas School Book Depository, fired one shot that missed and two more that caused all the wounds to JFK and Governor Connally.

The "Sniper's Nest"

The evidence and testimony below from the commission's account pinpoints the "snipers nest."

Howard L. Brennan was sitting on a concrete wall, facing the TSBD, about 120 feet (measured diagonally) from the southeast corner window on the sixth floor. Shortly after the assassination, he stated that he saw a man leave from and return to the area of the window a couple of times before the shots occurred. After the first shots he saw the same man aim a rifle and fire one last shot.[1]

Harold Norman, an "order filler" at the depository, was watching the motorcade from the window on the fifth floor directly below the southeast corner window on the sixth floor. He testified that he distinctly heard three shots, the sound of the bolt action, and shell casings hitting on the ceiling (sixth floor) above him.[2]

News photographer Bob Jackson riding in the eighth car of the motorcade, was facing the depository when the shots rang out. He told this author, "I heard three shots, but didn't know where to look until after the third. Then, I saw a rifle being pulled back inside the window that was right above the ones some black guys [undoubtedly one was Harold Norman] were looking out of."

Boxes of books were found stacked around that southeast corner window on the sixth floor.[3]

Three shell casings found close to the window confirmed that this was indeed the "sniper's nest."[4]

From the numerous evidentiary points that follow, one can only conclude that the man Howard Brennan saw firing a rifle from the southeast corner window on the depository's sixth floor was Lee Harvey Oswald.

And the Shooter Is...

In the evening on the day of the assassination, Howard Brennan identified Lee Harvey Oswald* as the person in a lineup who "most resembled" the man he saw firing in the window.

While at that time he did not "positively identify" Oswald,[5] on March 24, 1964, Brennan's testimony before the Warren Commission was much more meaningful. He testified that, "with all honesty," he could have positively identified Oswald out of the lineup, but did not want to do so fearing reprisals from any accomplices that he (Oswald) might have had. He explained that Oswald's death made any reprisals unlikely and enabled him to tell the truth to the commission about being able to positively identify Lee Harvey Oswald as the man he saw firing a rifle.[6]

Charles Givens, who had been working on the sixth floor before the assassination, testified that he saw Oswald holding his clipboard on the sixth floor about 11:55 A.M. (about 35 minutes before the assassination). Givens asked Lee if he were going to lunch. Oswald said "no" and asked him to close the elevator gate [so Lee could operate it from the sixth floor].[7]

Oswald's prints were found on some of the book boxes used to form the "sniper's nest."[8] Of course, because Oswald worked there, finding those prints was hardly a revelation; however, if his prints had not been found on those boxes, the commission's case would have been weakened.

Oswald's clipboard was found near the sixth floor stairway after

---

*For a chronology of the life of Lee Harvey Oswald, please see Appendix II.

the assassination. The clipboard indicated that he had not filled any book orders that morning.[9]

A 6.5mm Mannlicher-Carcano Italian rifle (C 2766) found near where his clipboard was found[10] matched one shown being held by Oswald in a backyard photo.[11]

Marina Oswald* testified that she took that "backyard" photograph.[12] Oswald had written on the back of the photo.[13] Experts determined that the photograph was taken with an Imperial Reflex camera belonging to Oswald.[14]

Oswald's palm print was found on that rifle.[15]

In 1993, Vincent Scalice, a leading fingerprint expert, used a "composite" of several photographs (each taken at a different exposure) of a fingerprint from near the trigger guard on the Carcano C 2766, to positively identify that print as belonging to Lee Harvey Oswald.[16]

Fibers from Oswald's clothing matched those found on the rifle.[17]

The FBI determined that Klein's Sporting Goods of Chicago had, on March 20, 1963, shipped a 6.5mm Mannlicher-Carcano rifle with scope to one A. Hidell, Post Office Box 2915, Dallas, Texas.[18] An order for that rifle had been received by Klein's on March 13, 1963. Oswald's handwriting matched that on the order form.[19]

The name A. J. Hidell was found on a list of persons authorized to receive mail at P.O. Box 30061, which had been rented by Oswald in New Orleans on June 3, 1963.[20] Marina testified that Lee used the alias Hidell in connection with his pro-Castro activities in New Orleans.[21] A Selective Service Notice of Classification and a Marines Certificate of Service bearing the name Alek James Hidell were found in his wallet.[22] Alex was the name Oswald used in Russia.[23]

Oswald admitted during questioning that he had rented P.O.

---

*On October 15, 1959, Lee Harvey Oswald arrived in Moscow, where he would reside until June 2, 1962. While there he met and later married Marina Prusakova, niece of the Soviet minister of internal affairs. After the Oswalds left Russia they lived together in the Dallas-Ft. Worth area, until Lee left on April 24, 1963, to try to find work in New Orleans. Marina, meanwhile, lived in the Dallas suburb of Irving with her friend, Ruth Paine.

Dillard Exhibit C

Figure 12: Enlargement of photograph taken by Thomas C. Dillard on
November 22, 1963

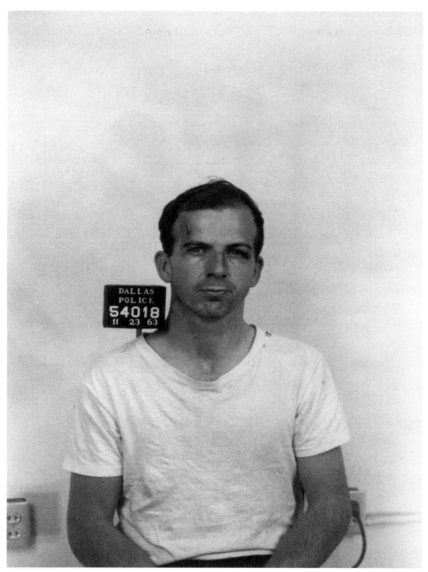

City of Dallas

Figure 13: "Mug Shot" photograph of Lee Harvey Oswald

Box 2915 in Dallas, to which the rifle had been shipped.[24]

A postal money order for $21.45, purchased in Dallas, was paid to Klein's Sporting Goods. Opposite the word "from" on the money order were written the words "A. Hidell, P.O. Box 2915, Dallas, TX.[25]

The serial number C 2766 on the rifle found near the "sniper's nest" matched the serial number on the rifle shipped by Klein's to Oswald.[26]

Oswald had gone to Ruth Paine's house on Thursday, November 21, 1963. It was unusual for him to go there on a Thursday because Friday was his normal visiting day (Marina and their two children were living with Ruth).[27] The rifle had been stored in Ruth's garage.[28]

Buell Wesley Frazier, a neighbor of Ruth's and coworker of Lee's, and Linnie Mae Randle, Frazier's older sister, both testified that they saw Lee carrying a package wrapped with brown paper while on his way to work on the morning of the assassination. Oswald told Frazier the package contained "curtain rods."[29]

That same morning, Lee left behind on his and Marina's bureau $170.00, which is nearly all the cash he had, and his wedding ring, the first time he had ever removed it. Both these touching acts were consistent with someone planning to do something that could cost him his life.[30]

An empty brown paper bag was found near the "sniper's nest."[31] Oswald's finger and palm prints were found on the bag.[32]

The bag contained brown and green fibers matching fibers in a green and brown blanket in which the rifle had been wrapped while stored in Ruth's garage.[33]

At 3:00 P.M. on the day of the assassination, a search of Ruth's garage showed the rifle to be missing.[34]

The entrance wound in the back of JFK's skull measured 1/4" by 5/8," which was consistent with being shot from behind by a 6.5mm bullet.[35]

The three shell casings found at the sniper's nest had been fired in Oswald's Mannlicher-Carcano rifle.[36]

Bullet fragments, recovered from the President's brain, were matched to a larger fragment (CE-567),[37] which was proven, to

Commission Exhibit No. 723

Figure 14: Shield of cartons around sixth floor southeast corner window

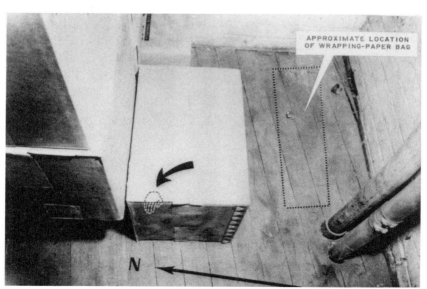

Commission Exhibit No. 1302

Figure 15: Approximate location of wrapping-paper bag and location of palm print on carton

Commission Exhibit No. 1303

Figure 16: The rifle

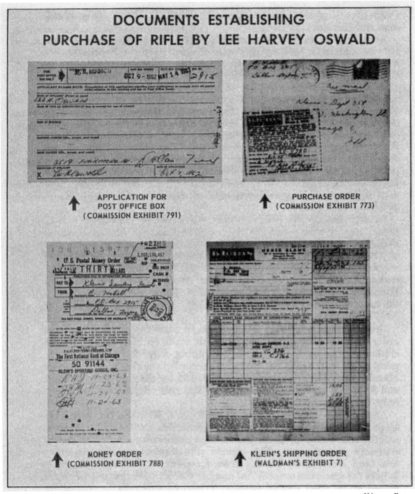

Figure 17: Documents establishing the purchase of the rifle
by Lee Harvey Oswald

Figure 18: "Backyard" photograph

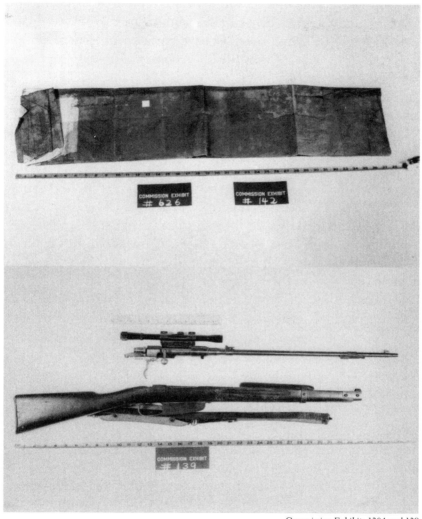

Commission Exhibits 1304 and 139

Figure 19: Top photograph is of a paper bag with tape measure shown below it. Bottom photograph is the rifle disassembled.

the exclusion of all other weapons, to have been part of a round fired from Oswald's rifle.[38]

The nearly whole bullet found on a stretcher at Parkland Hospital, thought to have caused the seven wounds to JFK and Governor Connally,[39] was proven to have come from Oswald's rifle.[40]

Oswald suspiciously left the TSBD approximately three minutes after the assassination.[41] Cecil J. McWatters, a Dallas bus driver, testified that Oswald boarded his bus near Dealey Plaza at about 12:36 P.M. (six minutes after the assassination) going to the Oak Cliff section of Dallas[42] (where Oswald's rooming house was located).[43] When arrested Oswald was carrying a bus transfer ticket confirming McWatters' story.[44] Mrs. Mary Bledsoe, Oswald's former landlady, testified that she saw Oswald get on McWatters' bus.[45] William Whaley, a cab driver, identified Oswald as the man he had driven to the Oak Cliff area from Lamar and Commerce[46] (about one block from Dealey Plaza).[47] Oswald admitted during interrogation that he initially took a bus from Dealey Plaza but caught a cab when the bus got stuck in traffic.[48]

Earlene Roberts, housekeeper at Oswald's 1026 N. Beckley rooming house, testified that Lee came home about 1:00 P.M., shortly after the assassination. She went on to say that he seemed to be in an "unusual haste." She remembered saying to him, "Oh, you are in a hurry," but Oswald didn't respond. She said he stayed only about three or four minutes and then left, taking his jacket.[49]

At least 12 persons saw a man with a revolver in the vicinity of where Officer Tippit was murdered immediately after the shooting. Six of those witnesses identified Lee Harvey Oswald in a police lineup as the man they saw. Three others subsequently identified Oswald from photographs as the man they saw, and two said he resembled that man.[50] The fact that Oswald committed this violent act is an indication that he was desperate, such as one might be if he had just shot the president. More evidence linking Oswald to Officer Tippit's murder includes:

Officer Tippit was murdered at the corner of 10th and Patton, only nine-tenths of a mile from Oswald's rooming house. The murder was recorded on police radio exactly at 1:16 P. M. If Oswald left his rooming house at about 1:04, as Mrs. Roberts said, he would have had time to walk to 10th and Patton and murder Tippit at 1:16.[51]

Barbara Jeanette Davis identified Oswald as the man she saw running across her lawn just after she heard gunfire. She also saw him eject empty shell casings from a pistol.[52]

When Oswald was arrested he was carrying a .38 caliber Smith & Wesson revolver.[53]

Cortlandt Cunningham, an FBI firearms identification expert, and Joseph D. Nicol, superintendent of the Illinois Bureau of Criminal Identification, tested four .38 caliber shell casings found at the scene of Tippit's murder and found that they were fired from the gun Oswald was carrying.[54]

Oswald was carrying five live .38 caliber cartridges in his pocket when he was arrested.[55]

Nicol matched one of the slugs recovered from Tippit's body to Oswald's .38.[56]

A .38 caliber Smith & Wesson revolver was ordered January 27, 1963, from Seaport Traders, Inc. by one A. J. Hidell.[57] It was established, as you recall, that A. J. Hidell was one of Oswald's aliases. Experts matched Oswald's handwriting to that on the order form.[58]

Johnny Brewer, manager of Hardy's shoe store, identified Oswald as the man he saw running and "ducking" into a recessed area in front of his store and then "duck" into the Texas Theater.[59] His rushing and "ducking" would be consistent with someone running to escape after committing two murders.

Mrs. Postal, who was selling tickets at the Texas Theater box office, testified that she saw Oswald "duck" into the theater without buying a ticket.[60] She was the person who called the police, leading to Oswald's arrest.[61] Again, the behavior of Oswald "ducking" into the theater without buying a ticket is consistent with someone trying to escape.

When Officer M. N. McDonald started to search Oswald as he was being arrested, Oswald said, "Well, it's all over now," punched McDonald in the face, and drew his revolver. McDonald struck back and grabbed Oswald's gun, both falling to the floor.[62] Lee's behavior was inarguably consistent with someone not only guilty of committing a serious crime, but also capable of taking another person's life.

Earlene Roberts, Oswald's housekeeper, testified that Lee was zipping up his jacket when he left the rooming house a few minutes after 1:00 P.M.[63] When Oswald was arrested he was not wearing a jacket. A jacket, which Marina identified to be Lee's, was found along the route from the scene of Tippit's murder to the Texas Theater where Oswald was arrested.[64]

A paraffin test was performed on Oswald's hands and right cheek at police headquarters. Lee tested "positive" (hands) for possibly firing a revolver but "negative" for firing a rifle (right cheek).[65] It should be noted that an FBI agent, who later fired three shots in succession from the Mannlicher-Carcano (C 2766), also tested negative for gunpowder residue on his right cheek.[66]

Oswald lied several times during his interrogation consistent with someone guilty of a crime. Some examples of his lying include:

He denied owning a rifle.[67]

He stated he bought a revolver in Ft. Worth when he actually ordered it from a distributor in Los Angeles.[68]

Commission Exhibit No. 143

Figure 20: Revolver used in Tippit killing

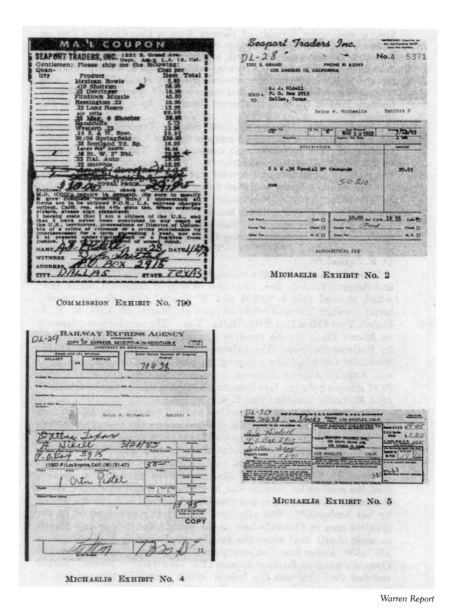

Warren Report

Figure 21: Revolver purchase and shipping documents

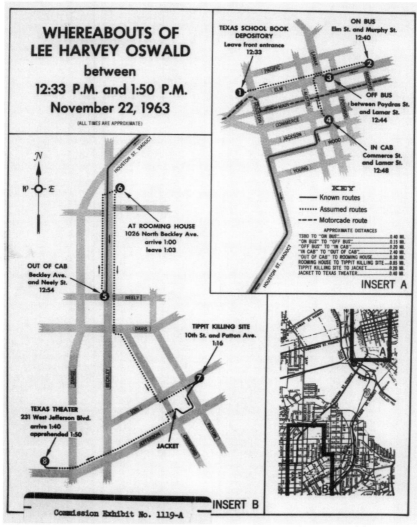

Commission Exhibit No. 1119-A

Figure 22: Whereabouts of Lee Harvey Oswald between
12:33 P.M. and 1:50 P.M. November 22, 1963

When asked if he knew an A. J. Hidell, he said no. He was then shown a Selective Service card from his wallet bearing that name.[69]

He denied that he ever told Buell Wesley Frazier that he wanted a ride to Irving (Ruth Paine's house) on Thursday, November 21 to get curtain rods for his apartment (in Dallas-Oak Cliff).[70] Frazier, however, testified that Lee did in fact ask him for a ride on that Thursday "to get curtain rods."[71]

He stated he never carried a package to the TSBD on the morning of the assassination.[72]

Lee stated he was having lunch with "Junior," a coworker, at the time of the assassination. James Jarman Jr. was the only employee called "Junior," and he testified that he neither ate lunch with nor even saw Oswald around the time of the assassination.[73]

Oswald told investigators that after the assassination he talked with Bill Shelley, a foreman at the TSBD, for about five or ten minutes and then went home because Shelley said there would be no more work. Shelley testified that he never saw Oswald after the assassination, and it would have been impossible for Lee to catch the bus when witnesses said he did if he spent even five minutes talking with Shelley.[74]

Oswald had absolutely no alibi for when JFK was shot.[75]

Besides murdering Officer Tippit and attempting to shoot another officer when he was arrested, Oswald's capability to kill [JFK] was also supported by the fact that he had attempted to murder* Maj. Gen. Edwin A. Walker, an anti-Communist activist, on April 10, 1963.[76]

There is no doubt that investigators handling the assassination

---

*Although Oswald was never even charged with attempting to murder General Walker, the evidence, which includes that listed below, is clear that he did.

1. After the assassination, photographs [of Walker's residence], which experts determined were taken on March 9 or 10, were found among Lee's possessions.[77] The experts also determined those photos were taken with an Imperial Reflex camera owned by Lee.[78]

2. Order forms and other evidence show that on March 12 he ordered a rifle.[79]

3. On April 10, about one hour after a shot was fired at General Walker, Marina found a note from Lee telling her what to do if he were either killed or arrested.[80]

of JFK, murder of Officer Tippit, and wounding of Governor Connally acted at times like "Keystone Cops" or even co-conspirators rather than professionals. They mishandled crucial evidence, violated Oswald's rights, and even covered up important details that they thought did not fit their case against Oswald. *The "untainted" and "uncontaminated" evidence remaining, however, is still overwhelming that Lee Harvey Oswald, as a lone gunman, did in fact assassinate President John F. Kennedy, wound Governor John Connally, and later murder Officer J. D. Tippit.*

The profoundly important question that remains is whether or not Oswald was part of an assassination conspiracy.

In chapter 3, I'll describe an event that I feel is inarguable evidence, showing more than anything else that there was no conspiracy to assassinate JFK. This event occurs only about two months before the assassination and will be the "foundation" of the case, which I'll build on in chapters 4 and 5, to show that no conspiracy existed.

---

4. At about 11:30 P.M., that same night, Lee returned home drenched with sweat and told Marina, "I shot Walker."[81]

5. A ballistics expert for the Warren Commission was unable to match a bullet fragment (CE-573) removed from Walker's residence to Oswald's rifle. He testified that, while the fragment was too smashed to make any kind of a match, the general rifling characteristics of the rifle are the same type as those on the fragment.[82]

6. In 1977, Dr. Vincent Guinn, using neuton activation analysis, concluded that it was "extremely likely" that CE-573 was from a Mannlicher-Carcano bullet.[83]

Note: The presentation in these chapters is not intended to chronicle the life of Lee Harvey Oswald. Actually, only the events occurring in his short life that best show he assassinated President Kennedy, but not as part of any conspiracy, will be detailed. For a more complete portrayal of Lee's life please refer to Appendix II, which contains a chronology of *The Significant Events in the Life of Lee Harvey Oswald*.

CHAPTER 3

No Conspiracy

On September 25, 1963, at about 12:20 P.M. Lee Harvey Oswald departed New Orleans bound for Mexico City.[1] He arrived at 10:00 A.M. on September 27.[2] Once in Mexico City he applied for a visa to travel to Cuba and then Russia.[3] He was turned down and departed Mexico City for Dallas on October 2 at about 8:30 AM.[4] On October 3 at about 2:20 P.M. he arrived in Dallas,[5] where he would spend the remaining 52 days of his short life.

Gerald Posner, in his brilliantly done *Case Closed*, pointed out that if Oswald had received the visa he applied for in Mexico City in late September 1963, *he would have been in Havana on the day of the assassination*. I don't believe Mr. Posner came close to sufficiently emphasizing the importance of this fact. Logically then, *if Oswald had received his visa, he would have been in Cuba on November 22, 1963 and there couldn't have been any conspiracy to assassinate the president (at least one at that point involving Lee)!* Be realistic. Not even Larry, Curley, and Moe would have plotted a conspiracy with their "main man" headed for the wrong country! Of course, I know that if any conspiracy theorists are still reading this book, they have two "counter arguments" left to hang on to. One is that Lee was only *"acting"* in Mexico City. If that were proven, I would be the first to agree that there probably was a conspiracy and Oswald was coming back to Dallas to assassinate JFK, regardless of whether or not his visa for Cuba was approved. Their other argument is that Oswald was being *"impersonated"* in Mexico City, and, as part of an even more complex conspiracy, either the real Oswald or another impostor was waiting to assassinate JFK. OK, I respect those two "counter arguments," which I will soon address, but meanwhile I hope you still agree that *if Oswald wasn't "acting" or being "impersonated" in Mexico City, he would have gone to Cuba (with an approved visa), and there couldn't have been a conspiracy (at least one at that point involving Oswald).*

Because of the somewhat lengthy discussion required, I thought it best to devote the next chapter, "Not an Act" to showing that Oswald was *not acting* in Mexico City. For now then, we are left with the question of whether or not he was being *impersonated* in Mexico City. The evidence on that issue speaks for itself and includes, but is not limited to, the following points:

1. Marina Oswald testified that Lee told her of his plan to travel to Mexico City.[6]

2. On September 17, 1963, he obtained a "tourist card" from the Mexican consulate in New Orleans. The name typed on the card was Lee, Harvey Oswald.[7]

3. A neighbor testified that on the evening of September 24, he saw Lee hurriedly leave his rooming house on Magazine Street, carrying two pieces of luggage, and board a bus.[8]

4. A Mrs. Twiford, whose husband was a member of the Fair Play for Cuba Committee, received a phone call at their Houston home, from someone by the name of Oswald around 10:00 P.M. on September 25.[9] He said he was a member of the Fair Play for Cuba Committee and that he wanted to talk to her husband before going to Mexico City.[10] Oswald's bus stopped that evening at Houston.[11]

5. Two British tourists, Dr. and Mrs. John B. McFarland, who boarded Continental Trailways bus no. 5133 in Houston (going to Laredo), testified that they talked to a man on that bus they later identified as Oswald, and that he told them he was going to Cuba.[12]

6. On a bus from Nuevo Laredo, Mexico going to Mexico City, two Australian girls, Pamela Mumford and Patricia Winston, said they talked to a man they later identified as Oswald. He told them that he'd been to Russia before and recommended a good hotel in Mexico City.[13]

7. Oswald registered in his own name at the Hotel del Comercio in Mexico City.[14]

8. Señora Silvia de Duran, a Mexican citizen employed at the Cuban embassy stated that Lee Harvey Oswald visited there on Friday, September 27.[15]

9. Lee's visa application included his photo and had his own signature.[16]

10. Three employees of the Soviet embassy all confirmed that Lee Harvey Oswald visited their embassy on September 27.[17]

11. Ernesto Lima Juarez stayed at the Hotel del Comercio in Mexico City the last few days of September through the first few days in October 1963. He identified Oswald from photos as being the man he saw at the hotel while he was a guest there.[18]

12. A hotel maid and night watchman also identified Oswald as staying at their hotel.[19]

13. A waitress at a small restaurant adjacent to the hotel identified Lee Harvey Oswald as being the man she served several lunches to. She said, "He ate the soup of the day, rice, and either meat or eggs, but refused dessert and coffee." [20]

14. Marina testified that after Lee returned, he showed her postcards depicting bullfights and other attractions and described actually attending a bullfight.[21]

15. Investigators found notations he had made in a Spanish-English dictionary and on a guide map of Mexico that were among his possessions.[22]

16. A month after his trip, Lee wrote to the Soviet embassy in Washington, criticizing officials at the Cuban embassy in Mexico City for "grossly breaching regulations" and for being "unprepared." [23]

Hopefully, you are now as convinced as I am that the "real" Oswald did travel to Mexico City, and that there was no "impersonator." In the next chapter, we'll see that Lee Harvey Oswald, without a doubt, was *not acting in Mexico City and really tried to travel to Cuba, not back to Dallas!*

CHAPTER 4

Not an Act

The importance of whether or not Lee Harvey Oswald was acting in Mexico City when he tried to go to Cuba and Russia cannot be overstated. This is because, and I'm repeating myself for emphasis, *if he wasn't acting, and was granted the visa he wanted, he'd have been in Havana on November 22, and it is unreasonable to believe that there was any conspiracy to assassinate JFK (at least one at that point involving Lee Harvey Oswald).*

Basic to determining Oswald's sincerity in Mexico City is whether or not he was a true Marxist Communist. In other words, the idea of his sincerely trying to go to Cuba and Russia is substantially easier to accept if it is shown beyond any reasonable doubt that he truly embraced the social and political systems of those two countries. While the instances of Lee demonstrating his Marxist Communist inclinations throughout his short life are numerous and well documented, four in particular clearly show this allegiance to be genuine.

Instance 1: Lee displayed an interest in Communism while in junior high school.[1] Surely at this young age he wasn't acting as part of some assassination conspiracy. Besides that, JFK had not even been elected president at that time.

Instance 2: Soon after Lee first defected to Russia and found out that he was about to be sent back, he attempted suicide. Because his self-inflicted wounds were so severe[2] it's illogical to think that his defection was part of some conspiracy or anything else besides a genuine effort to live in Russia and be part of a Communist society.

Instance 3: On April 10, 1963, Oswald attempted to assassinate retired Maj. Gen. Edwin A. Walker,[3] a Dallas anti-Communist activist. The gravity of such an act demonstrates Oswald's deep and resolute pro-Communist allegiance.

Instance 4: During a filmed debate in New Orleans with Edward Butler, an anti-Communist activist, Oswald was totally unsuspecting and surprised when Butler talked about Oswald's "hardship" discharge from the Marine Corps, defection, and Marxist Communist affiliation.[4] Oswald, cornered, became emotional and stated he definitely was a Marxist! View that footage when Oswald made that remark, and if he is lying (or acting) he should be posthumously presented an Academy Award!

I believe those four instances serve well to confirm that Lee's true political inclinations were consistent with someone who sincerely wanted to go to Cuba and Russia. In addition, there are numerous instances where his behavior reveals the intensity of his desire to go to those Communist countries. I've listed three such instances.

Instance 1: While still in New Orleans, Lee concocts a "crazy" scheme in which he and Marina hijack an airplane and go to Cuba.[5] Oswald is so serious he has a written operational plan for this nonsense that had himself in the cockpit controlling the pilot, and Marina, with a gun, controlling the passengers. Marina talks him out of the idea by telling him the passengers would never understand her "English."[6] This was all Marina's testimony, but why would she make up a story like that? Logically it's true, and shows that Oswald sincerely wanted to go to Cuba and then Russia, supporting the idea that he was not acting in Mexico City!

Instance 2: When he was turned down for a visa by the Cubans in Mexico City, he all but literally had to be tossed out of the Cuban embassy.[7] Furthermore, Sylvia Duran, an embassy employee who had tried to help Oswald with his application, stated that, when he was told his application was disapproved, he was "red" and "almost crying."[8] Should we get out another Academy Award or just agree that he wasn't acting!

Instance 3: At the Soviet embassy, a Soviet official (actually KGB) Oleg Nechiporenko, stated that Oswald, trying desperately to get his travel authorized to Cuba and Russia, was "in tears" when told he wouldn't be able to travel to Russia.[9]

The above is evidence that Oswald was not acting in Mexico City and therefore really was trying to go to Cuba, not back to Dallas, to be part of a conspiracy to assassinate JFK. Admittedly, though, what is not "totally" ruled out, is the "unlikely" possibility that Lee could have been selected, after his return from Mexico City, to participate in a previously born conspiracy. That possibility, however, should be eliminated given the points presented in chapter 5, "Points of No Conspiracy." These "points," like so many "nails in the lid of an old wooden coffin," should allow all conspiracy theories to "rest in peace!"

CHAPTER 5

Points of No Conspiracy

By now I hope you are convinced that Lee Harvey Oswald was trying to go to Cuba only seven weeks before the assassination of JFK. I hope you're also convinced, based on that alone, that the chances of his being involved in a conspiracy are minimal at best. However, many conspiracy theorists wouldn't change their mind on this issue if Oswald's ghost appeared and begged them to believe he was a "lone" assassin. Nonetheless, for the open-minded, the following "points of no conspiracy" should close the case on the conspiracy issue once and for all!

Ruth Paine drove from her home in Irving and arrived in New Orleans on Friday, September 20, 1963. She took Marina and the Oswalds' daughter little Junie back to stay with her in Irving while Lee was supposed to go to Houston or Philadelphia to look for work.[1] Before they left, Lee had wrapped his rifle in a greenish-brown blanket and packed it with their other possessions in Ruth's station wagon.[2] *There's no evidence to show that Lee saw that rifle again until the night before the assassination.* It had been stored, and never unwrapped from the blanket, in Ruth's garage from late September until November 21. Here's the point. If a conspiracy existed, perhaps rivaled in historical significance by only the one which felled Julius Caesar, wouldn't someone have checked, at least once in eight weeks before the assassination, to make sure the rifle hadn't been rendered inoperable by being dropped, or run over by a lawnmower, or even worse, removed? Some conspiracy!

Anyone running a conspiracy to assassinate the president of the United States would surely have wanted their triggerman "tuned up" (practicing with his rifle and adjusting his scope) for the big day. That would be somewhat difficult though if he hadn't even seen his rifle for eight weeks. Either this was one pretty poorly run conspiracy, or just maybe, there wasn't one!

It's doubtful that conspirators would have enlisted a "nut" like Oswald to be the "triggerman" in an assassination of this magnitude. Let's face it, Oswald was three french fries away from being a "Happy Meal!" We're talking about someone who was planning to hijack an airplane. That's not even to mention that he went to Russia to be part of their "sweatbox" society, tried to commit suicide, tried to assassinate a major general, and then tried to go to Cuba to "work for" his hero, Fidel. Few who knew about him could be certain whether he was pro-Castro or anti-Castro. Some believed he was on the CIA's payroll. Also, many at that time didn't know for certain whether or not Lee was an FBI informant. So, Lee probably wouldn't have been at the top of the "World's Most Desirable Assassins" list. In fact, let's give any alleged conspirators some credit...they wouldn't have gone near someone as peculiar or unpredictable as Oswald!

With regard to Oswald needing practice, it shouldn't be forgotten that he was "0 for 1" at that point, in assassination completions (he missed trying to kill General Walker on April 10, 1963). For the record, that shot at Walker was less than 100 feet in distance with a 4X power scope. Going back to the previous point about alleged conspirators choosing Oswald as their shooter, wouldn't "they" have chosen someone with a better "assassination record?" There's a simple explanation for that. There was no conspiracy!

Now, Lee Harvey Oswald may have been called a "nut," but does anyone think he would have been stupid enough to accept a "hit" assignment from conspirators powerful enough to assassinate the president of the United States? In other words, conspirators such as these would surely "hit" the "hit man" as soon as he had completed "his business." Let's give Lee just a little credit for having some common sense and realizing that if he "hit" President Kennedy as part of some conspiracy, he'd be signing his own death warrant! No conspiracy!

Would conspirators plotting the assassination of JFK have wanted their hit man to murder someone else, especially someone as prominent as General Walker only seven months before he was supposed to kill the president? What if he'd been caught? Go to "plan B?" To those who still insist there was a conspiracy, at least admit that, with lousy planning like this, they were lucky!

One more reference to the Walker assassination attempt. Evidence shows that Lee meticulously planned this attempt for about two months. In fact, he compiled a "military-like" operational plan including photos of Walker's house, maps, and notes. In addition, he buried his rifle ahead of time near the Walker residence so he wouldn't have to carry it on the night of the attempt.[3] He had also written a somewhat lengthy letter to Marina on what to do if he were caught or killed after the attempt.[4] What I'm driving at here is, why would Oswald do all that planning and preparation to kill a general and hardly any to assassinate the president of the United States? The answer is, he didn't have time to make an operational plan because he didn't even decide to do it until a day or two before the assassination. That also points to "no conspiracy!"

Before Lee was hired at the Texas School Book Depository, he applied at Padgett Printing Co. He was turned down only at the last minute because one of his references, Jaggars-Chiles-Stovall, was checked and they recommended not hiring him.[5] Padgett was several blocks from the eventual motorcade route[6] so, if there was a conspiracy, there are three possibilities as to what the "conspirators" were up to, and those are: *One*, they were so impressed with Oswald's shooting ability, they were going to let him get hired at Padgett so he could shoot a simple "cross city" shot at the president; *Two*, he was "acting" and really didn't want the job; *Three*, and lastly, conspirators were going to let him get hired, and then have him quit and get the book depository job later. All three possibilities are a little far-fetched for me. The truth is that if Padgett had hired him, like they almost did, JFK would probably have been reelected in 1964! How could there have been any conspiracy?

Oswald's employment along the eventual presidential motorcade route was actually a tragic coincidence of monumental proportions rather than part of a conspiracy plan. Let me explain.

Oswald, recently back from New Orleans (and Mexico City) was looking for work in the Dallas area. One of Ruth Paine's neighbors, Mrs. Linnie Mae Randle, told her that her younger brother, Buell Wesley Frazier, had recently been hired at the book depository and that they might still be hiring. Ruth phoned the depository on Lee's behalf and set up an interview for him. Roy Truly, the superintendent, decided to hire Lee not so much because he needed more workers, but mainly because Lee was a former GI and out of work. Truly had two possible positions for Lee. One was in a storage warehouse across town and the other, of course, was at the main depository. There's no doubt whatsoever in my mind that if Truly had put Lee to work at the storage warehouse, JFK wouldn't have been assassinated on November 22, 1963! Truly, however, opted for letting Lee work at the main depository on Elm Street;[7] and you know the rest. Now, if there was a conspiracy, were Truly, Ruth Paine, Buell Wesley Frazier, and Mrs. Randle all in on it? Once again this incident doesn't fit the conspiracy "story line" very well!

Lee used his real name when he rented a room at 621 Marsalis in the Oak Cliff section of Dallas.[8] That wouldn't be the most prudent thing to do for a person involved in a conspiracy to assassinate the president! "No" on any conspiracy!

Ruth Paine began giving Lee driving lessons on October 13, 1963. She gave him his last lesson on November 11.[9] Evidently, he thought his driving skills were good enough to get his license, so on November 9, he and Ruth went to the driver's license examination office. It was closed, however, due to its being a local election day.[10] He tried again on Novovember 14, but the line was too long and he left.[11] Lee must have been getting even more confident about his driving because Clifton M. Shasteen, an Irving barber, testified that Lee drove Ruth's car to his shop to get a haircut.[12] Albert Bogard, a car salesman at Downtown Lincoln-Mercury, stated that Oswald test drove one of the cars on his lot. Bogard later passed a lie detector test when the FBI questioned his story.[13] Buell Wesley Frazier supported Bogard's story by telling the Warren Commission that Lee told him he was planning to buy a car.[14] In addition, Edward Brand, an insurance salesman, told the FBI that Lee had inquired about buying auto insurance for a car he was going to buy.[15] The question is why, if there was a conspiracy going on, would he go through all that trouble and expense, shortly before the assassination, of learning to drive, getting his license, and buying a car? Alas, conspiracy critics have this figured out.... Lee was simply going to drive his car from Dealey Plaza after the assassination. Well, poor planning, at least in my humble opinion. With his limited driving experience he probably wouldn't have gotten very far without having a wreck, especially if high, "getaway" speeds or driving through heavy downtown Dallas traffic were necessary. I'm sorry, I just can't see how Lee's learning to drive and buying a car, just before the assassination, fit into any conspiracy plot. Is it more likely that Lee wasn't planning at this time to assassinate JFK (no conspiracy), but was simply trying to improve himself as a husband and father, or simply make it easier in the future to find work?

If a conspiracy of this proportion were being plotted, surely the conspirators would have planned for more than "one" shooter, such as in a "crossfire." In concert with that thought, many critics have argued that there was at least one shot from the front, proving that there was a conspiracy. They seem to be about evenly divided, however, on whether the shot or shots came from the grassy knoll and/or an Elm Street storm drain. Both locations offered shots that were so easy, a first-time shooter could have scored a hit. Interestingly though, the ballistic, scientific, and medical evidence is overwhelming that all the wounds to the president and governor were caused by two bullets,[16] fired from the Mannlicher-Carcano found on the sixt floor of the depository.[17] The evidence does not support the existence of any grassy knoll or "storm drain" shooter that would prove that there was a conspiracy.

If the ballistic, scientific, and medical evidence aren't enough to permanently quell the theories that there was a shot from the front, consider this point. Every bullet fragment, including those recovered from JFK's brain and Governor Connally's wrist, and those found under the jump seat and on the front seat, as well as the bullet residue from the inside of the windshield molding, was discovered in locations *even with* or *in front of* where JFK was sitting. Pray tell this author how the rounds from which these fragments and residue came, were shot from the front! I've heard of "frangible" and "explosive" bullets, but not "bouncing" bullets! Be assured that there was no frontal shot, much less any conspiracy.

Surely, in a conspiracy of this magnitude wouldn't there be a "backup" shooter? I mean, what if Oswald couldn't get the shot off? In fact, five men had been laying new plywood on the sixth floor of the depository on the day of the assassination. They had left the sixth floor and were taking their lunch break when the motorcade passed. What if the motorcade was a little early, or late? Those five men may well have have been back on the sixth floor laying plywood. Despite the boxes of books shielding the sniper's nest, that work crew would have had ringside seats to perhaps the most important murder in history! You wouldn't have to be a world class assassination planner to pick a better spot to place your shooter than possibly in front of a gallery of workers! This lack of any evidence that there was a backup shooter plus the poor location for a "sniper's nest" means there's a doubtful existence of any conspiracy!

Oswald had rented a room at 1026 N. Beckley on October 14. According to his landlady and roommates he never received or made any phone calls except to Marina.[18] His landlady told investigators that he stayed in his room 95 percent of the time.[19] This would be rather peculiar behavior for a shooter or one of the shooters involved in an assassination conspiracy! Wouldn't he need to practice with his rifle or cover assassination details with his co-conspirators? I thought the author of one book I read had kind of a neat explanation for that question. He said Oswald crawled out through the window in his room to attend assassination meetings. Doesn't wash, no conspiracy!

On November 1, Lee sent in his membership fee to join the ACLU.[20] Why would he do that if, as part of some conspiracy, he was going to assassinate JFK in three weeks? The answer is, at that time, he had no idea whatsoever he'd murder JFK. There was no conspiracy!

On the same day, November 1, Lee rented a post office box through December 31, that year.[21] Now, you have to know that

Lee was a notorious "penny-pincher"[22] who was so miserly that, rather than buying his own trash can, he put his trash in the neighbor's.[23] He also tipped well. When he used a taxi to escape Dealey Plaza, the fare was 95 cents. He gave William Whaley, the cabbie, a dollar bill for a "whopping" tip of five cents![24] The point is, why would someone this cheap waste money renting a box past the time he was going to be either killed or captured after trying to assassinate JFK? Conspiracy theorists might say that maybe Oswald was planning to get away (and continue to live in Dallas). Wrong! The correct answer is, when he rented the box he wasn't planning to assassinate JFK. No conspiracy!

Ten days prior to the assassination, Lee mailed a letter to the Soviet embassy in Washington, D.C. In it he asks to be informed as soon his and Marina's Soviet entrance visas arrived.[25] Either he was acting once again as part of a conspiracy or he was really trying to go back to Russia. I say he was trying to go to Russia. No conspiracy!

Evidently, it was on that same day, Tuesday, November 12, when Oswald walked into the Dallas FBI office and asked if agent Hosty was in.[26] Agent Hosty maintained the file on Oswald (because of his Communist-related activities), and, in the course of checking up on him, had twice been to Ruth Paine's house in Irving where Marina was staying. Hosty wasn't in, but Lee handed the receptionist a note for her to give him. It was written in an angry tone and basically said that Hosty shouldn't bother Marina again or else Oswald would take appropriate action. Hosty swore that the note was unsigned, however both agent Kenneth Howe and receptionist Nanny Fenner, stated that it was indeed signed by Oswald.[27] This author finds it remarkable if not negligent that, after receiving such a note from a known Communist just days before the president's visit, agent Hosty didn't at the very least "shadow" Oswald until JFK had departed Dallas. The point is, if there was an assassination conspiracy in motion, how could the plotters possibly have relied on Hosty *not to keep a close eye on Oswald?* Once again, the explanation that makes the most sense is that there was no conspiracy!

If, let's say, factions from within the CIA and/or "military industrial complex" had colluded to assassinate JFK, their sinister plans would surely have included recruiting a reliable if not professional hit man. An assassin of this caliber would be expected to take full advantage of the element of surprise and make the first shot count. In Dealey Plaza, however, on that tragic November day, it was actually a piece of street curbing some 280 feet from the presidential limousine that felt the first round. By all rights the sound of that misaimed shot should have triggered instant practiced protective measures by Secret Service agents. In fact, the second round wasn't fired until three-and-one-half seconds after the first, more than enough time to "cover" the president and/or accelerate his limo out of harm's way. Sadly, what should have happened did not, and in this author's opinion the practically comatose reactions ["I thought it was a firecracker"] from Secret Service agents cost President Kennedy his life. In any case, that wild, "miss the entire barn door" first shot which should have resulted in a botched assassination was obviously not the signature work of a CIA-recruited professional assassin, but that of a lone oddball named Lee Harvey Oswald firing his $19.95, WWII-vintage rifle.

One of the most popular conspiracy theories features a "second" Oswald who supposedly was recruited and trained by the CIA or KGB to take the place of the "real" Oswald and assassinate JFK. Actually, the practically continuous whereabouts of the Lee Harvey Oswald born in New Orleans on October 18, 1939, from probably as far back as high school until just before his death, could be easily traced. Indeed, Lee's handwriting on the numerous notes and letters he wrote throughout those years (this evidence is preserved in the National Archives) begs authentication by those seriously seeking the truth about the existence of any "second" Oswald. Adding motivation for such an endeavor is the fact that even the best forgeries from that time would be routinely exposed by the handwriting experts of today. Predictably, however, Lee's notes and letters will be left undisturbed, at least by proponents of this particular conspiracy theory. They know of course that the results of any such handwriting analysis would clearly prove there was never any Oswald impersonator, much less one involved in a conspiracy to assassinate President Kennedy.

Some conspiracy theorists maintain that no one helped Oswald escape because conspirators wanted him to get caught. In other words he was being set up as a patsy. I have a problem with that theory. Even if Lee was framed as masterfully as anyone in history, I don't believe for one minute that conspirators would have allowed him to be captured and risk the possibility of his helping authorities track them down. It makes better sense that they would have silenced Oswald immediately after the assassination, or, as an alternative, provided a better means of escape than a "footmobile," bus, and taxi. As you may know, Lee was caught easily and stayed alive for nearly two days after the assassination. Highly doubtful on any conspiracy!

If there was a conspiracy, was it just poor planning that resulted in Oswald murdering a Dallas police officer during his "getaway" practically right in front of a dozen witnesses? A much more likely explanation is that, besides Lee himself, there were no planners.

The exact motorcade route wasn't published until November 19.[28] The fact that conspirators would have had, at the most, only a few days to plan how, when, and where their "shooter" or "shooters" should be positioned, and the fact that Oswald started working at the book depository on October 16,[29] on their own merit seem to make conspiracy theories fall apart like cheap watches. Critics counter this point, however, by insisting that conspirators somehow either "set up" or found out about the motorcade route long before it was published. What these critics should know is that *no one*, including the Secret Service, Dallas Police, and even the White House knew the route until November 14.[30] As far as having conspirators "on the inside" setting up the route, it was Governor Connally* who, more than anyone else, was respon-

---

*The motorcade route could not be determined until a site was chosen for the Dallas luncheon. Prior to November 14 it hadn't been decided whether to hold the luncheon at the Trade Mart, a few minutes drive northwest from downtown Dallas, or the Women's Center to the southeast of Dallas, but a little further away than the Trade Mart.[31] If the Women's Center had been the final choice, the motorcade would have proceeded from Dallas' Love Field heading south then east through Dealey Plaza on Main Street (with no sharp turns to slow for) and onto the fair grounds where the Women's Center was located.[32] It should be added that, had the motorcade been heading east, Jackie Kennedy, sitting to the president's left, would have obstructed the line of sight between him and the Elm Street area. As history sadly reflects, however, the Trade Mart was the final choice for the luncheon site, and on its way there the motorcade passed slowly (negotiating the 90 degree turn from Main onto Houston, and the 110 degree turn from Houston onto Elm) through Dealey Plaza, heading west. Many critics in hindsight (which has always been 20-20), claim that the motorcade could have avoided the sharp, ill-fated Main-Houston-Elm turns by staying on Main Street and "jumping over" a small concrete divider separating Main and Elm. There is no question that this maneuver,[33] which Dallas locals made routinely (and "illegally"), would have provided the motorcade access directly from Main Street to the Stemmons Freeway, which led to the Trade Mart. Nevertheless, it was agreed by the Secret Service and Dallas Police that the motorcade should comply with traffic regulations and utilize Houston and Elm Streets to reach the freeway. Getting back to the critical selection of the luncheon site, it had been originally decided on November 6, by Ken O'Donnell, JFK's appointments secretary (and "right hand man") that the Trade Mart was inappropriate for the luncheon.[34] Mainly there were two problems with the Trade Mart. One was a series of "catwalks" overhanging where the luncheon tables would be set up. Any "hecklers" or unwanted demonstrators on those catwalks would be difficult to remove, disrupting the luncheon and embarrassing the president. The other was that the building's several floors or tiers, made it more difficult to secure.[35] Disregarding these problems, the governor insisted that the luncheon be held at the Trade Mart.[36] There has been no shortage of conjecture as to why Governor Connally was so adamant about having the luncheon in a building that, seemingly, was not suited for a luncheon of this nature. Some believe that he realized the new and modern Trade Mart building would be more acceptable to Dallas' "wealthy elite,"[37] and their financial backing would greatly benefit the Democratic committee. Others have speculated that, because of an ongoing feud between the "conservative" governor and "liberal" Texas senator Ralph Yarborough,[38] the governor planned to sit with the president and vice president at a luncheon table on one tier and have Yarborough sitting with individuals of lesser importance at a separate table on another tier.[39] It should be noted that the Women's Center had only one floor and did not offer the governor an opportunity to have the senator seated on a different level. Whatever Governor Connally's motives were, Ken O'Donnell "acquiesced" to his wishes,[40] and (reversing the decision he made on November 6), on November 14 made the selection of the Trade Mart as the luncheon site final.[41] In retrospect, had Ken O'Donnell not bent to the governor's pressure, the motorcade would have sped straight on Main Street through Dealey Plaza, heading east towards the Women's Center, and there can be little doubt, that the course of history would not have been dramatically altered such as it was on November 22, 1963.

sible for the motorcade route being finalized at such a late date and also for it passing directly in front of the Texas School Book Depository.[42] With his five wounds, the governor would have been the last person on earth, behind JFK himself, to be involved in an assassination conspiracy! But why aren't those important facts brought out in the hundreds of conspiracy novels that have been published? The answer is that information of this nature contradicts if not totally "blows apart" the sensational and better selling but fictional theories these authors present. Clearly there was no conspiracy.

It had been raining in Dallas up until about midmorning on the day of the assassination.[43] For just such occasions the president's limousine was outfitted with a removable, clear plastic* "bubbletop."[44] Ken O'Donnell, from his hotel room in Fort Worth, had passed instructions to secret service agents in Dallas, "If the weather is clear and it's not raining, have the bubbletop off."[45] By about 10:00 A.M., a gloomy overcast gave way to bright sunshine.[46] Shortly thereafter, secret service agent, Forrest Sorrels had the bubbletop removed as instructed.[47] Had it continued to rain that bubbletop would have stayed on and, in all likelihood, JFK would have departed Dallas alive and well. The point here is, considering that inclement weather had been forecast for the Dallas area for November 22, any conspirators, surely knowing that when it's raining the bubbletop goes on the president's limo, would have postponed their evil deed for a better day. There was no conspiracy, only incredibly bad luck and a "nut case" with a rifle. History will never reflect an instance when rain was needed more than it was in Dallas, for just a few hours around noon, on November 22, 1963.

Critics insist that dozens of individuals, who may have died under somewhat unusual or even "suspicious" circumstances were actually "silenced" to ensure an assassination plot wasn't exposed. These same critics, however, might be hard pressed to explain

---

*The plastic was neither bulletproof nor bullet-resistant.[48] Nonetheless, if closed, the reflections and decreased visibility would have made the presidential target many times more difficult to hit.

why not one of these "murders" has ever been solved and positively linked to any assassination conspiracy.

For any conspiracy to be successful, it would have been necessary to recruit scores of qualified "traitors" to accomplish numerous sinister tasks including, but not limited to: (1) planning and coordinating each phase of the conspiracy, (2) finding out (well in advance) the motorcade route, (3) ensuring that Oswald was hired in the depository, (4) planting evidence in and around the "sniper's nest," in the limo, at the scene of Tippet's murder, and at Parkland Hospital, (5) firing at the president in concert with Oswald and/or other assassins, (6) removing telltale cartridges and bullet fragments from rounds fired by "other" assassins, (7) "doctoring" numerous photographs, (8) falsifying the autopsy and ballistics and neutron activation test results and dozens of documents related to the cover-up, and (9) "silencing" certain witnesses and/or participants. It's simply incomprehensible that, in 36 years, aside from the Warren Commission and House Select Committee on Assassinations, hundreds of enthusiastic and dedicated (if not obsessed) researchers and dozens of amply financed investigative reporters for CBS' *60 Minutes*, *20-20*, *Hard Copy*, *Unsolved Mysteries*, *Time*, *Newsweek*, *The Enquirer*, etc. would not have flushed out and "broken the silence" of even one out of so many conspirators. Surely the first plotter to be convinced the conspiracy might unravel would be hell-bent to cut an "immunity for evidence or information" deal with authorities. Then before you could say "let's make a deal," each involved in the treacherous scheme would turn on the other, causing the entire conspiracy to collapse like a house of cards. Nothing of the kind, however, has collapsed, and the best explanation for that is, of course, that there was no conspiracy! Perhaps though, it is somewhat less horrifying that, instead of a powerful cabal from within our own government, it was a lone, twisted wretch named Lee Harvey Oswald who assassinated President Kennedy.

A point made by Dr. Michael Baden, chairman of the HSCA's forensics panel (regarding the question of whether or not any conspiracy existed), has some similarities to my previous point but deserves to be included here:

The variety of conspiracy theories had called into question every bit of evidence, including the body itself. According to one scenario, during the plane ride from Dallas to Washington the entrance wounds were altered to look like exit wounds in order to confuse everyone about the direction of the shots. According to another, the original autopsy report, photographs, and x-rays had all been stolen from the National Archives and replaced with fakes. I wondered at the vast numbers of people that would have been required to carry out all these tasks and the extraordinary combination of luck, competence, and intelligence, so lacking in all other human endeavors, that would have been needed to pull off these delicate and complex conspiracies in secret—and have them remain secret.

One final point. *If there was a conspiracy, where is the hard, physical evidence, e.g. another weapon, bullet fragments or casings from a weapon other than Oswald's rifle, etc.? There has never been one piece of hard evidence presented that shows there was a conspiracy. In fact, the only "evidence" of a conspiracy in 36 years has been hearsay or less than irrefutable statements and testimony from "witnesses." There was no conspiracy, but unfortunately, what has been written on the subject mostly reflects one assassination plot or another. While some authors sincerely believe their conspiracy theory is a true account, many others intentionally conjure up high-intrigue, sensational, supposedly nonfiction work solely for profit. It is this exploitation that must cease and desist, once and for all, not only out of respect for the memory of President Kennedy and for his family, but also so that the currently ambivalent written record on one of the most important events in history can be made more definitive and representative of the facts and evidence.*

Many conspiracy theorists believe that because Jack Ruby's murder of Oswald had all the characteristics of a "mob hit," then there probably was a mob conspiracy to assassinate JFK. What they don't consider is the possibility that *Oswald assassinated JFK on his own,* and then was "silenced" for reasons not having a whole lot to do with JFK's assassination. As a matter of fact that's what I believe really happened, and I'm going to tell you how and why it happened in Part II, "The Mob Silences Lee." Before that though, there's a "loose end" that needs to be taken care of, and that is Lee's "motive." I've told you there was no conspiracy, so if Oswald wasn't enlisted or hired by conspirators, he must have had his own motive. This is explored in the next chapter, "Lee's Motive."

CHAPTER 6

Lee's Motive

If Lee Harvey Oswald had been involved in some conspiracy to assassinate JFK, there would be little concern for his motive. The usual reason a "hit man" does his dirty deed is for money. Well, there was no conspiracy, therefore Lee must have had his own motive. Because we obviously cannot get into his head to see what he might have been thinking when he decided to kill President Kennedy, we can only speculate as to his motive.

Before getting into Lee's motive, however, I have an opinion, actually about murders in general that might be appropriately mentioned here. I believe, given the same set of circumstances, a person who owns a weapon is much more likely to commit or even consider murdering someone than someone who doesn't own a weapon. This would be valid even if the weapon was purchased for perfectly innocent reasons, e.g. home protection, hunting, target shooting, etc. There are two reasons for my belief.

First, those who already own a weapon have an "option" available to them on how to resolve a problem, should one arise, that they wouldn't otherwise have. For instance, let's say a man who owns a rifle that he bought for deer hunting is threatened by his neighbor over some obviously serious dispute. Our man must consider his options on how to handle the problem (and threat). His options include notifying authorities, ignoring his neighbor altogether, simply trying to "appease" his neighbor, and, because he owns a rifle, using it to intimidate or even shoot his neighbor. The point is that, if he didn't already own a rifle, because the process of purchasing a firearm can be somewhat involved, shooting his neighbor probably wouldn't be included in his options.

Second, most murders are committed on impulse. If the period of time, starting from the moment a person first decides to commit murder until they have their first opportunity to carry out that decision, is increased because that person has to go out and purchase a weapon, there's a better chance they will "cool off" and reconsider the decision.

So, what does all that have to do with Oswald's motive for assassinating JFK? I believe that while there were other factors, of course, that contributed to Lee's deciding to assassinate JFK, one was the fact he already owned a rifle. Indeed, it was a sad twist of fate that Oswald actually bought that rifle to assassinate General Walker, not JFK! It is my belief that Oswald first considered killing the president on either the 19th or 20th of November, when he read in the newspaper in the book depository first floor lunch room,[1] that on November 22, JFK's motorcade would pass directly in front of his workplace. He must not have mulled too long whether or not to kill the president, because by about 10:00 A.M. on Thursday, November 21 his plan to kill JFK was in motion. That's when he asked Buell Wesley Frazier for a ride home from work to Ruth Paine's in Irving[2] (where his rifle was stored). I'm convinced that if Lee did not already own that Mannlicher-Carcano rifle, there's absolutely no significant chance that he would have gone out and purchased a rifle and assassinated JFK.

Another factor, I believe, was that Lee was distraught and bitter towards society in general. Whether he was in America or Russia, his feelings seemed to be the same. Actually, for America, Lee had nothing but disdain. For anyone, though, familiar with Lee's background and struggles in life, that should come as no revelation. His father died two months before his birth. His mother, Marguerite, was dominating and extremely difficult to live with. By 1956, Lee had moved 21 times.[3] He had been in and out of 12 different schools.[4] His family was poor and he had few of the nice things his peers had. In the Marines he had been court martialed, incarcerated, and "undesirably" discharged. In Russia he found that the "grass wasn't any greener," and came back to the U.S. Back in America he was ridiculed for his political beliefs, and jailed. Frequently harassed by the FBI, he had been evicted, fired several times, and had to move often to find work. Even the Cubans wouldn't allow him to go to their country. Save possibly David Ferrie (to be introduced shortly), he had no real friends or close associates. He was unable to provide well for his family and they separated from him. To say that Lee Harvey Oswald was distraught and bitter would be a gross understatement! That indeed was the Lee Harvey Oswald who, on November 22, 1963, struck back at the society which he believed had dealt him a bad hand by assassinating the one person who he felt best represented that society, John F. Kennedy.

Still another factor that may have contributed to Lee's lethal actions on November 22, 1963, was that he blamed, at least partially, President Kennedy for "foiling" his greatest dream—of going to the country of his hero, Castro. Evidently he blamed the president for not being able to travel to Cuba, because he was told by Cuban embassy officials that the reason his visa for Cuba was disapproved was that "the U.S. Government didn't allow Americans to travel to Cuba." In fact he had been told correctly, because on January 3, 1961, the U.S. broke off all diplomatic relations with Cuba and officially banned travel to that country on January 16, 1961.[5] Ironically, though, President Eisenhower, not Kennedy was responsible for the ban on travel to Cuba. Nevertheless, Lee blamed JFK. There is some evidence to support this. It comes from one of the FBI's most trusted sources, code-named "SOLO." SOLO was actually comprised of Jack Childs, the U.S. Communist Party's financial adviser, and his brother Morris, former editor of the Communist publication *Daily Worker*. They informed for the FBI but were trusted by Castro. After the assassination a secret memo to FBI director Hoover stated that Castro had told SOLO that, "When Oswald was in the Mexico City Cuban embassy, and told that the U.S. Government didn't allow Americans to travel to Cuba, he said 'I'm going to kill Kennedy, I'm going to kill that bastard.'"[6] Obviously, that memo isn't absolute proof that Oswald threatened JFK. I believe, however, that it is likely that Oswald did make a "threatening" statement like that. I believe that because it makes sense! First, why wouldn't the Cuban embassy officials tell Oswald about the "U. S. Government banning travel" after they disapproved his visa? After all, they would have been correct. It also makes sense that Lee would blame and, considering his temper, threaten President Kennedy for a U.S. Government policy that prevented him from going to Cuba. On November 19 or 20, when he made his decision to kill JFK, I believe, at least in part, he was carrying out the threat he made in Mexico City.

Certainly though, when one tries to determine what motivated Lee to assassinate JFK, the possibility that he was trying to avenge or stop the attempts to assassinate his hero, Fidel Castro, must be considered (much more on this, including who was responsible for and how Lee found out about the plots to kill the Cuban dictator, will be discussed in Part II).

The last major factor that I believe contributed to Oswald's decision to assassinate JFK was the unbelievably easy opportunity to do so, that fate seemed to drop right in his lap! For example, from where Lee was working at the time, all he had to do was to hit a nearly stationary target no further than about 88 yards away (it appeared as if it were only 22 yards with his 4X scope).[7] The opportunity to assassinate JFK presented to Oswald was tailor-made.

In conclusion, I believe Lee Harvey Oswald was trying to get even with a society that he thought was responsible for making his life miserable, by killing JFK, who not only was the person that best represented that society, but also prevented him from going to Cuba. The attempts on the life of Castro may also have been significant. In addition, he already owned a weapon quite suitable for what he planned to do, and the opportunity couldn't have been much easier!

In Part I, I believe I've presented a convincing case that Lee Harvey Oswald, alone, assassinated President John F. Kennedy.

In Part II, we'll see how and why the Mob silenced Oswald on November 24, 1963.

PART II

THE MOB SILENCES LEE

About Part II

Every account on the subject that I'm familiar with, whether written or on video, links Lee Harvey Oswald's assassination of JFK with Jack Ruby's murder of Oswald. These accounts either theorize that both Oswald and Ruby were part of a conspiracy or that they were both "lone" gunmen. In this regard, *Silencing the Lone Assassin* is different. While you know that I believe Oswald was a "lone assassin," I also believe and intend to show in Part II that Jack Ruby "silenced" Lee Harvey Oswald on behalf of the Mob, *but for reasons unrelated to the assassination!* Admittedly, however, the case I present here will be somewhat "speculative," certainly in contrast to the case I presented in Part I. The reason is simply that there is less evidence and fewer facts available, relating to Oswald's murder, as compared to JFK's assassination. There are three "causes" for this lack of evidence. *One*, because of Lee's ties to Communism, the government feared that any assassination conspiracy uncovered might involve Russia or Cuba and could possibly lead to World War III. So understandably, they set the course of the investigation towards a "lone assassin" conclusion (luckily they were correct) and away from any leads that even hinted of a conspiracy. Ergo, to not conflict with that conclusion, their probing of Jack Ruby's motives and connections was shallow and conveniently resulted in a determination that he murdered Oswald on behalf of no one. Consequently, in my showing the opposite, i.e. that Ruby was hired by the Mob to silence Oswald, it has to be done without the best possible information base, compliments of the Warren Commission. *Two*, as you'd expect, the Mob didn't exactly lay down an obvious trail of evidence that could incriminate them. And *three*, over the course of the 36 years since the assassination, many fabrications repeated over and over have emerged disguised as facts, making it difficult to sort out the truth from what is not. Also, many key witnesses are deceased. Nonetheless, I will reconstruct the scenario and major events leading to Jack Ruby's "silencing" of Oswald as logically and accurately as I possibly can based on the available evidence and the facts that I felt were most significant.

CHAPTER 7

Oswald in the Big Easy

On April 24, 1963, Oswald departed Dallas and arrived in New Orleans early in the morning of the 25th. With him he had 50 Fair Play for Cuba leaflets.[1] Lee's main effort at this time was devoted to building a "portfolio," containing information that would help him get to Cuba and even impress Fidel once he was there.

I Want to Help Fidel

There were *two* ways that Lee intended on building his portfolio and helping Castro. *One,* was the obvious: pro-Castro, high-profile activities which included handing out literature such as *Hands Off Cuba* handbills and denouncing JFK's policy towards Cuba at street demonstrations and student gatherings on the campus of Louisiana State University at New Orleans.[2] The other way was "infiltrating" the anti-Castro Cuban exiles in and around New Orleans who were trying to oust Castro and his Communist regime from Cuba. He believed that Castro would need and want to know what these exiles were up to. To accomplish that he posed as someone who was anti-Castro and soon became involved with the exiles, who it turned out were "Mafia connected" (the Mafia wanted Castro out of Cuba as much as the Cuban exiles so they could get back their lucrative casinos). Three key characters Lee became involved with while infiltrating the exiles are listed below. A brief background of each is included.

Guy Banister: Banister, a former FBI agent, was anti-Communist and ran a detective agency out of an office at 544 Camp St., New

Orleans. This office had been characterized as the Grand Central Station for Cuban exile activities. Reportedly, Banister was "intimately connected" with the CIA's anti-Castro activities in New Orleans. Some have said Lee Harvey Oswald occasionally used a small office upstairs from Banister's main office to run his Fair Play for Cuba Committee affairs.[3] If this is true, there can be little doubt that the radically anti-Communist Banister was duped by Oswald into believing he was also anti-Communist, and only masquerading as a pro-Castro activist in order to ferret out true pro-Castro sympathizers. It's likely that Oswald's former Civil Air Patrol commander, David Ferrie (introduced next), who worked for Banister, recommended Oswald [to Banister]. In 1963, Banister did investigative work for Carlos Marcello (to be introduced shortly). Considering his ties to Ferrie, Marcello, the FBI, and the CIA, it's highly likely that Banister knew all about the CIA-Mafia Castro assassination plots (to be discussed later).

David Ferrie: Ferrie was a former Marine and pilot for Eastern Airlines before he was fired for his homosexual activities. Ferrie worked not only as an investigator for Guy Banister at 544 Camp St., but also for Wray Gill, attorney for Carlos Marcello, the powerful Mafia chieftain (his background follows). Ferrie allegedly flew Marcello back to the U.S. after Bobby Kennedy had him deported to Guatemala. Reportedly, at Carlos' request, he flew Vincent Marcello (Carlos' brother) back and forth on "business trips" between New Orleans and Dallas.[4]

Ferrie was a member of the Marcello-backed Cuban Revolutionary Council, an anti-Castro organization headed by Sergio Arcacha Smith. It is believed that Ferrie's association with Marcello may have developed out of their mutual accociation with Smith.[5] Moreover, Ferrie spent time with Marcello not only at Carlos' office at the Town and Country Motel but also at his Churchill Farms estate, supposedly to plan strategy on how to beat the INS' charges against him.[6] As a reward for helping him win the INS case, Marcello financed a gas station franchise for Ferrie.[7]

Ferrie admitted to the FBI that he had made "threats against JFK," blaming him for the failure of the Bay of Pigs invasion of

Warren Commission

Figure 23: Oswald distributing *Hands off Cuba* handbills in New Orleans,
August 16, 1963

Cuba in 1961. He went on to say that he really didn't really mean
the threats. A witness testified (during the Garrison trial of Clay
Shaw), however, that he even drew out a "triangulation" diagram
to show how shooters should be positioned to assassinate the President.[8] Ferrie also was a member of a paramilitary group called the
Anti-Communist Brigade (INTERPEN).[9] Other members of
INTERPEN included Gerry Patrick Hemming, a former Marine
and operative for the Office of Naval Intelligence,[10] and Frank
Sturgis,[11] a CIA contract agent who would later be well-known for
his role in Watergate.[12]

Considering his association with Banister, Marcello, Hemming,
and Sturgis, there can be little doubt that Ferrie learned all about the
CIA-Mafia plots to assassinate Castro (discussed later in this chapter).

Ferrie was an officer in Lee Harvey Oswald's Civil Air Patrol
unit.[13] The evidence is strong that during the summer of 1963
Ferrie met with Oswald on several occasions, one of which was
reportedly at an anti-Castro exile training camp in Lacombe, Loui-

siana.[14] This author believes that Oswald not only misled* Banister but also Ferrie, convincing them both he was anti-Castro and that his pro-Castro activities were helping him infiltrate and identify pro-Castro activists.

Carlos Marcello: Carlos was the Mafia don of a billion-dollar-a-year empire that was based in New Orleans and covered all of Louisiana and Texas.[15] The *Wall Street Journal* once stated that Marcello was wealthier than Rockefeller.[16] Despite his current wealth, he (as well as certain other Mafia chieftains) had grand ambitions of regaining control of the lucrative casinos in Havana that Castro had expropriated shortly after he came to power in 1959. For those ambitions to be realized, though, they would first have to oust Castro from power. To that end, Marcello's efforts were not insignificant. He contributed heavily to Cuban exile leaders participating in the Bay of Pigs invasion in 1961.[17] In addition he had made an agreement with the exiles whereby he would support them financially in return for them giving him casino rights should they be successful in retaking Cuba from Castro.[21] Marcello had originally made the "funding for casino rights" agreement with Sergio Arcacha Smith, who was head of the Cuban Revolutionary Council (CRC), a fund-raising front for the anti-Castro exiles. While Smith was removed as CRC leader in Janu-

---

*While the fervently pro-Castro Oswald was successful in convincing Banister and Ferrie that he was anti-Castro, at least one member of the New Orleans anti-Castro community saw through his facade. That alert individual was Carlos Bringuier. On August 5, 1963, Oswald visited Carlos' store and told him he'd like to join the anti-Castro struggle. Lee even gave him a Marine guerrilla warfare manual. From the outset, however, Bringuier was suspicious that Oswald was really pro-Castro.[18] On August 9, Carlos' suspicions were strengthened when two of his friends told him they saw Lee handing out pro-Castro literature on Canal Street. Bringuier then sent his friend Carlos Quiroga to Oswald's home to try to find out one way or the other whether Lee was pro- or anti-Castro.[19] While Quiroga was there, Marina and little Junie Oswald started speaking Russian. When Carlos noticed, Lee explained that he had been taking Russian speaking classes at nearby Tulane University. Later, after Bringuier found out that Oswald was lying about taking classes at Tulane, he was more sure than ever that Lee was pro-Castro.[20]

ary 1962,[22] and the exiles around New Orleans dispersed after their Lake Pontchartrain training camp was raided by the FBI on July 31, 1963, there is no reason to believe Marcello discontinued funding their operation. Nothing had changed regarding his aims to control the lucrative casinos in Havana. It wasn't, however, until the mid to late 1970s that it became known just how serious Marcello had been about achieving those aims. In 1974 it was reliably reported to Warren Hinckle and William Turner, coauthors of *Deadly Secrets*, that Marcello offered $100,000 to Sam Benton, a Mafia wheeler and dealer, in return for his arranging Castro's assassination.[23] Moreover, in 1979 Marcello told undercover FBI agent Joseph Hauser that he had been involved in the CIA-Mafia plots to assassinate Castro[24] (these plots, hatched from late 1960 to 1963, will be explained in more detail a little later in this chapter). Separate from the CIA-Mafia schemes, a "new" CIA plot to assassinate Castro went into motion in September 1963. It is likely that Marcello was at least aware of the new plot, code-named AM/LASH. While Marcello had been trying to help "remove" Castro, the FBI and Robert Kennedy (U.S. attorney general) had been seemingly relentless in their efforts to convict and imprison or deport him. Making matters even worse, the INS prosecuted him for falsification of immigration documents and perjury. On April 4, 1961, Marcello was totally humiliated when Bobby Kennedy had him plucked off the streets of New Orleans and deported to Guatemala without even a suitcase or change of clothes. It's no wonder then that Marcello once said, "If you cut off the head (John Kennedy), the tail (Robert Kennedy) stops wagging!"[25] Marcello and David Ferrie were close associates, as Ferrie's investigative efforts helped Carlos beat the INS charges against him.[26]

Lee has Connections

Lee's "infiltration" of the anti-Castro groups around New Orleans was made easier by the fact he previously knew David Ferrie, who reportedly had risen to be second in command of the New Orleans anti-Castro, paramilitary men.[27] Ferrie was Lee's Civil Air Patrol instructor in 1955.[28] In addition, when Lee was a Marine stationed near Biloxi, Mississippi, he spent his weekends in New Orleans (90 miles west of Biloxi) and may have furthered his relationship with Ferrie.[29] In the words of Jim DiEugenio, a student of the assassination for about 25 years and author of *Destiny Betrayed*, "There is no debate about Ferrie's relationship with both Oswald and Banister."[30] And yet, an Oswald-Ferrie association is disputed by many non-conspiracy theorists such as the notable Gerald Posner (*Case Closed*). Mr. Posner in fact refutes the testimony of literally every witness who said Oswald and Ferrie were even acquainted. Nevertheless, I have compiled and listed below what I call "Points of an Oswald-Ferrie Association" to support my contention (and that of many before me) that Oswald and Ferrie were indeed associated, and perhaps even friends. It should be noted that the credibility of some of the individuals listed is questionable. But the fact that there is so much supporting information in itself seems to confirm the existence of such an association.

Points of an Oswald-Ferrie Association

1. Photographs are available that clearly show Oswald and Ferrie together at a Civil Air Patrol (CAP) picnic in 1955.[31]

2. Edward Voebel, a friend of Oswald's in the CAP, stated that he believed Oswald attended a party at Ferrie's home after a CAP ceremony.[32]

3. Frederick O'Sullivan, a detective with the New Orleans police department, told the FBI that Oswald first attended meetings at the CAP's Lakefront Airport squadron and later at their Moisant Airport unit.[33] Interestingly, Ferrie had been the squadron commander at not only the Lakefront but at the Moisant Airport unit as well.[34] What is especially significant, though, is that both Oswald and Ferrie changed squadrons (Lakefront to Moisant) at about the same time![35]

4. This author had the pleasure of speaking personally with John B. Ciravolo, who was a member of the Moisant CAP unit in 1955. He stated that he remembers quite well that Oswald was also a member and that Ferrie was the unit's commander.[36]

5. Daniel Powers, a fellow serviceman of Lee's, reported to the Warren Commission that while Lee was assigned to the Marines

near Biloxi, Mississippi, he would take the bus to New Orleans literally every weekend.[37] This has led to speculation that Oswald was spending at least some of his time in New Orleans with Ferrie.[38]

6. Delphine Roberts, Guy Banister's secretary, told Anthony Summers (*Conspiracy*) that Oswald walked into her office and filled out the forms to be one of Banister's "agents." Later, she went on, Banister called Oswald into his office and the two had a lengthy "closed-door" meeting. She continued, saying, "As I understood it, he had the use of an office on the second floor."[39] Mrs. Roberts' daughter (also named Delphine), who used an office upstairs from Banister's, told Summers that she and a "photographer" friend both saw Oswald occasionally and that he had his pamphlets and books "along from where we were."[40] Ferrie worked in Banister's office.[41]

7. Daniel Campbell, a young former Marine hired by Banister, told Summers he saw Oswald in Banister's office.[42] Again, Ferrie also worked for Banister in that office.[43]

Courtesy John B. Ciravolo, Jr.

Figure 24; This 1955 photo shows David Ferrie (second from left) and Oswald (far right) at a Civil Air Patrol camp near Alexandria, Louisiana. John Ciravolo, who was kind enough to talk with this author about the assassination, is shown standing in front of Oswald.

8. Perry Russo, a longtime friend of David Ferrie's, testified that Oswald was at a party with Ferrie. Dr. Esmond Falter and Dr. Nicholas Chetta (New Orleans coroner), who were both qualified to use the truth serum sodium pentothal and hypnosis administered both to Russo and concluded he was telling the truth.[44]

9. A number of Oswald's Fair Play for Cuba committee flyers and pamphlets were found in Banister's office by his widow.[45] Ferrie worked in Banister's office.[46]

10. Oswald had the address "544 Camp St., New Orleans" printed on a number of his pro-Cuba fliers. On top of that, letters written by Oswald were found indicating that he had used an office in New Orleans.[47] Ferrie worked at that address.[48]

11. Ferrie went to Oswald's former rooming house right after it was announced that Oswald was a suspect in the assassination.[49]

12. Ferrie, suspiciously, took off in the direction of Dallas only a few hours after Oswald was captured and being held there as a suspect.[50]

13. Banister's 544 Camp St. office was described by Sergio Arcacha Smith, an anti-Castro exile leader, as being the "Grand Central Station" for exiles,[51] and for the arms smuggling "underground railroad" reaching from Dallas to Miami.[52] It simply makes sense that if Oswald were trying to "dig up" information on anti-Castro activities, 544 Camp St. would have been high on his list of places to find this information. Ferrie worked at that office.[53]

14. After Banister's death, authorities found a file titled "23-7, Fair Play for Cuba Committee" in his 544 Camp St. office. A state police officer stated he saw the contents of that file and that it contained basic information on Oswald's activities.[54] Ferrie worked in that office.[55]

15. Ferrie was a very active member of the violent right-wing cadre of anti-Castro paramilitary men in and around New Orleans. Some even said he had risen to second in command.[56] Doesn't it make good sense that if Oswald were gathering information about anti-Castro activities, he'd try to "get close" to Ferrie?

16. Oswald worked at Reily Coffee Co., just around the corner from 544 Camp St.[57] Again, Ferrie worked at that office.[58]

17. Michael Kurtz, professor at Southeastern Louisiana Uni-

versity, stated in his book that he saw Oswald and Banister sitting and talking together in Mancusso's restaurant adjacent to 544 Camp St.[59] Ferrie worked for Banister.[60] This author had the honor and privilege of interviewing Professor Kurtz. To this day and to the letter he stands by what he wrote.

18. Reportedly, Oswald accompanied Ferrie to an anti-Castro exile training camp in Lacombe, Louisiana, near New Orleans.[61]

19. Jack Martin, a private detective who worked for Banister, told investigators for New Orleans District Attorney, Jim Garrison, that Ferrie and Oswald were associates and that he believed Ferrie taught Oswald how to fire a rifle with a telescopic sight.[62]

20. Edward Whalen, a friend of Ferrie's from Philadelphia, told Garrison investigators that Ferrie had spoken to him about Oswald.[63]

21. Adrian Alba, who ran a garage near 544 Camp St., told the Warren Commission that Oswald frequented Mancusso's restaurant[64] adjacent to 544 Camp St. where Ferrie worked.[65]

22. David Lewis, who worked for Banister, told Garrison that he thought he might have seen Oswald and Ferrie together not only in Mancusso's restaurant, but in Banister's office as well.[66]

23. William Gaudet, who reportedly worked for the CIA for more than 20 years, told Anthony Summers that he'd seen Oswald with Banister near his office, which was only a "stone's throw" from Banister's 544 Camp Street office. He also said Ferrie was with Oswald.[67]

24. In Clinton, Louisiana, numerous reliable witnesses identified Oswald and Ferrie as two men who, with another man, had visited their town late in the summer of 1963.[68] The registrar of voters, Henry Palmer, said Oswald showed him proper identification. Town barber Edward McGehee said he cut Lee's hair.[69] The House Select Committee on Assassinations concluded that the six witnesses from Clinton indeed gave "credible and significant" testimony as to the visit to their town by Oswald, Ferrie, and another man.[70]

I Trust You, Lee

By midsummer, 1963, Lee surely had gained the complete trust and confidence of his longtime associate Ferrie and was able to gather a "windfall" of information from him on New Orleans anti-Castro activities that might even impress Fidel when Oswald reached Cuba. The information Oswald received from Ferrie was "startling" and probably included the location of the exiles' arms caches and training camps. In fact, several accounts tell of Oswald accompanying Ferrie to an anti-Castro exile training camp in Lacombe, Louisiana, not far from New Orleans.[71] Oswald also must have learned that Banister's office at 544 Camp Street was the "Grand Central Station" of the illegal arms flow to the exiles.[72] There can be little doubt, though, that the most volatile piece of information Ferrie must have told Lee was that the CIA and Mafia (including Marcello) had been conspiring to assassinate Fidel Castro. On the surface an alliance between the CIA and Mafia may seem quite awkward, but after considering that they had a mutual enemy (Castro), perhaps one could make some sense out of such a coalition. While the CIA obviously wanted to rid Cuba of Castro and Communism, the Mafia wanted Castro out just as badly so they could get back their casinos. The plotting actually began in the fall of 1960 when a high-ranking CIA official met with Robert Maheu, a former FBI agent who had Mafia connections, John Roselli, a Las Vegas underworld figure, Sam Giancana, the Mafia leader of Chicago, and Santos Trafficante Jr., the Florida Mob boss.[73] Born from that meeting was the plan for Roselli to pass "CIA supplied" poison pills to a Cuban (a close associate of Castro who later turned traitor and befriended Trafficante), who would "administer" them to the unsuspecting Cuban leader.[74] The "Cuban," however, evidently lost his position in the Castro government before he could administer the pills.[75] Nonetheless, the CIA-Mafia plotting continued (with several more attempts being made to assassinate Castro) until at least January 1963. Supposedly that's when the CIA finally decided it might be unwise to continue "doing business" with the Mob.[76] It is likely, though, that it wasn't until later, probably even after JFK's assassination, that the Mafia (including Marcello) and Ferrie realized the CIA had dissolved their partnership with regard to trying to assassinate Castro.

While Oswald must have been looking forward to telling Fidel what the exiles around New Orleans were up to, and about the CIA-Mafia assassination plots, he seemed recklessly oblivious to the fact that it could be quite dangerous for anyone to possess information of this nature. Powerful individuals and forces, including senior CIA officers and the Mafia (including Marcello) wouldn't think twice about silencing anyone who might be a threat to disclose information about their assassination schemes to authorities.*

Certainly by mid-September, '63, Oswald had cunningly "milked" his old associate, albeit an unwitting David Ferrie, out of all the information on anti-Castro activities he thought he'd need to get to Cuba and help his hero, Fidel. Ironically, this information, that he was planning to use in Cuba was the reason he would soon be "silenced" by the Mob!

---

* Only two months after the CIA-Mafia assassination plots were first conjured up (August, 1960),[77] the schemers had thrown caution to the wind by allowing the FBI to find out from a wiretap, that "Maheu was up to something with Giancana,"[78] and evidently it had to do with the assassination of Castro.[79] Perhaps, though, the indiscreet assassination plotters were lucky. Their careless disclosure to the FBI had occurred while the plots were only in their embryonic stage, certainly months before any actual assassination attempt would be made. They had brushed with Hoover's "G-men," and while their tail feathers had certainly been singed, their clandestine operation had not been shot out of the sky. Much wiser, from then on they would conduct their monumentally ill-conceived affairs far more discreetly. The first attempt to assassinate Castro was made on February 13, 1961, when poison pills intended for Fidel were passed from the CIA to Roselli.[80] Meanwhile the FBI in all probability was certain only that the CIA and Mafia had been planning the assassination of Fidel Castro (Hoover "allegedly" sent RFK a memo to that effect on May 22, 1961).[81]

How the FBI first found out about the CIA-Mafia debacle is an interesting and somewhat humorous story, perhaps worth taking the time to recount.

Around the time the CIA and Mafia were beginning to plan their assassination of Castro, Sam Giancana asked Robert Maheu if he could arrange the "bugging" of Dan Rowan's suite at the Riviera Hotel in Las Vegas (Rowan had been appearing with his partner Dick Martin in their comedy duo). The purpose of the bug was to ascertain whether or not Giancana's girlfriend Phyllis McGuire (of the well-known singing trio, the McGuire Sisters), was having an affair with Rowan. Maheu agreed to help and employed Miami private eye Ed DuBois to place a sensitive microphone on the wall of the room next to Rowan's suite. Since the wall wouldn't be penetrated, there would be no "breaking and entering," and the "bug" would be legal. DuBois' operative in Las Vegas, Arthur Zalletti, however, planted numerous listening and spying devices, including an "illegal" tap on Rowan's phone.[82] Just as if Maxwell Smart himself had planned the fiasco, a maid easily discovered some of the electronics and notified the local sheriff, who in turn notified the FBI. After the FBI collected a wide assortment of eavesdropping gadgets and arrested Zalletti, they played back tapes of conversations that had been recorded. The federal crime busters must have been stunned to hear the voice of Giancana himself discussing how the Mob was conspiring with the CIA to assassinate Castro.[83] Consequently, (although they curiously didn't bring up the assassination plots) the FBI questioned Maheu about Giancana. The ex-FBI agent promptly asked his friend, Sheffield Edwards (a CIA officer who was also in on the plots) to intervene on his behalf.[84] The FBI evidently listened to Edwards, because just as if nothing had happened, Maheu went back to working on the plots.

Nevertheless it wasn't until May 7, 1962, that the record reflects that the attorney general was fully informed by the CIA about the plots. On that day CIA officers Lawrence Houston and Sheffield Edwards met with RFK and officially informed him that the CIA had collaborated with the Mafia for the purpose of assassinating Fidel Castro.[85] Why the same attorney general who brought more convictions against organized crime figures than perhaps any leader of the Justice Department in history didn't prosecute those involved in these assassination schemes when he had the chance can only be speculated upon. For this author there are three plausible reasons that might explain why RFK failed to act. One, if details of these mindless plots became known to the public, the damage to the government's credibility would be severe. Moreover, it could have been a political disaster. Two. There were many "in the loop" who felt that RFK not only condoned the plots but supported them as well. That contention was spawned from the fact that he did not specifically tell CIA officers Houston and Edwards, when they informed him about the plots, that they would not be permitted to ever collude with the Mafia again in such ventures. Instead, RFK simply told them, "If you even try to do this business with organized crime again, you will inform the attorney general."[86] And three, RFK may well have been hamstrung to prosecute the schemers because Sam Giancana, who played a key role in the plots, was a threat to expose scandalous information he possessed about President Kennedy. That "dirt" Giancana possessed was about two of JFK's extramarital affairs. One was a relatively brief but intimate relationship with Marilyn Monroe.[87] The other was a much longer and more involved affair with another shapely and sexy actress, Judith Campbell.[88]

Not being specific as to the reason he "applied the brakes" to the wheels of justice at a time when they should have been rolling over those involved in one of our government's most moronic breeches of the law since its birth, what

RFK said to FBI director Hoover (shortly after the May 7, 1962 meeting with Houston and Edwards) was profoundly telling. He said, "It would be difficult to prosecute Giancana or Maheu now or in the future!"[89]

With all that being said, one might ask the somewhat obvious question, "Why would it be dangerous for Oswald to possess information about the plots if RFK had known about them for months, and, if the Mob's 'blackmail card' would protect them from prosecution anyway?" The answer to the first part of the question is that, even though the Mob had their assumptions, it is highly improbable that they were ever certain the attorney general was aware of their scheming with the CIA, much less the fact that they actually attempted to kill the inconvenient Cuban leader. The answer to the second part is, if authorities at various levels and the media were to find out about the plots, whether from Lee or anyone else who had significant information that could be substantiated, the affair would have received immediate, intense, and widespread national attention. Certainly RFK would have bent to the resulting pressure to mount a full investigation into the matter, regardless of Giancana's "blackmail card" or any other reason that kept him from doing so earlier. Few if any would have been excluded from prosecution.

CHAPTER 8

The Assassin's Fate is Sealed

With his portfolio in hand, which must have been filled with information about his pro-Castro activities and accomplishments, operations of the anti-Castro Cuban exiles, and, most important, the plots to assassinate Castro, Lee departed New Orleans on September 25, 1963, for Mexico City. As you recall, in Mexico City he had hoped to secure a visa to go to Cuba. It is important to point out that Ernesto Rodriguez, who claimed to be a former CIA agent on assignment to Mexico City in September, 1963, stated that *Oswald told Soviet and Cuban embassy officials there, and even local reporters, that he had information about a plot to assassinate Castro.*[1] Regardless of Lee's assurances that he had vital information for Castro, due to the U.S. government's "ban on travel" to Cuba imposed on January 16, 1961,[2] his visa was disapproved. Embittered, angry, distraught, and alone, he left Mexico City bound not for Cuba as he had hoped, but for Dallas, where he would spend the remaining 52 days of his life. (For your reference, Appendix II contains a chronology of Lee Harvey Oswald's life.)

On November 22, 1963, at 12:30 P.M. CST, President John F. Kennedy was assassinated. Most in the world were shocked and sad, but some expressed much different emotions.

My God, It's Oswald!

In a New Orleans federal courtroom on November 22, 1963, at about 1:30 P.M., the trial of Carlos Marcello for charges including conspiracy and perjury[3] was interrupted by an announcement that "President Kennedy is dead."[4] David Ferrie was with Marcello and they both must have be thrilled at the news. Their longtime nemesis, JFK, was dead! Then at 1:45 P.M., court was recessed for jury deliberations.[5] It's not unlikely that during the recess Marcello and Ferrie had access to a television. At about 2:45 P.M., Ferrie's emotion had to have gone from exuberance over the death of JFK to one of total disbelief and paranoia when he saw that Lee Harvey Oswald had been arrested for the murder of Dallas police officer J. D. Tippit and was a suspect in the assassination! Incredibly, just a few months before that Ferrie had divulged to Oswald the innermost secrets and details about the activities of the exiles and CIA-Mafia plots to assassinate Castro.

This is Going to be Difficult!

Ferrie had the unenviable task of telling Marcello that he had told the same Lee Harvey Oswald, now in the custody of Dallas police, *information that, if given by Oswald to authorities, could, trigger the indictment of those involved in the plots to assassinate Castro, including Marcello and Trafficante, not to mention several high-ranking CIA officials.* For Carlos, that meant the attorney general and FBI, who had been trying relentlessly since early 1961 to get any kind of a conviction they could against him, might finally have the information they needed to put him away. Marcello feared that with the death of JFK turning Giancana's blackmail card from an ace into a deuce, the Justice Department would not hesitate to go after the Castro assassination plotters (including certain CIA officials, Robert Maheu, and underworld figures Roselli, Giancana, Trafficante, and himself).

Whatever the circumstances, Carlos Marcello wasn't about to risk losing his billion-dollar-a-year empire by giving a pathetic waif like Oswald a chance* to talk to authorities. His reply to Ferrie's admission about telling Oswald things he shouldn't have prob-

---

* It's not unlikely that Carlos would have been motivated to silence Oswald, not only to protect himself from prosecution but also Trafficante, either just because they were friends or on a "quid pro quo" basis. Also, besides making sure that he and Trafficante weren't prosecuted, Marcello may have had another reason for keeping Oswald from "spilling his guts" about the CIA-Mafia plots. Carlos might have believed there was still some chance, even if slight,

ably were words to the effect of, "We've still got time here to 'set something up' with Joe" (Joe Civello was Marcello's "underboss" in Dallas).[6] At that point, about 3:00 P.M., one of Carlos' "boys" must have made a beeline for the nearest pay phone to call "Joe."

In Dallas

Jack Ruby** probably received the "request" to hit Oswald from Civello or an associate no later than about 3:15 P.M. It is important to note that Bill Cox, an officer at Jack Ruby's bank, stated that at about 3:30 P.M. Ruby showed up[7] with close to seven thousand dollars in cash.*** What seemed strange to Cox is that, besides carrying that much cash only three hours after the president

---

that the CIA and Mafia team could take out Castro and help keep his hope of getting casino rights in Havana alive.

** For a chronology of the life of Jack Ruby, please see Appendix III.

*** While Ruby was carrying $7,000.00 only three hours after the assassination, he had $2,000.00 on him at the time of his arrest. In addition, another $10,000.00 was found in the trunk of his car and in his apartment.[8] The source of all this cash is unclear, however, there is a possibility that Ruby, who, supposedly had been tagged the "western kingpin of an arms smuggling corridor extending eastward through Louisiana to Miami," had recently profited from a gun running deal. Supporting such a theory is the existence of an FBI report that stated, on November 19, 1963, only five days after a National Guard Armory in Terrell, Texas, was burglarized, a member of the U.S. Army stationed at Terrell, Samuel Baker, paid Ruby a large sum of money.[9] Could that money have been Ruby's "cut" for setting up a "buy" for weapons that Baker stole from the Terrell armory? If that were true, it might explain why Ruby had so much cash during the weekend of the assassination. Consistent with the notion that Ruby was involved in the smuggling of arms are three more facts. One, when authorities searched Ruby's apartment they discovered, in a storeroom, a case of hand grenades, several M16 rifles, a Browning Automatic Rifle (BAR), and several thousand rounds of ammunition.[10] Two, in September, 1963, the FBI reported that an associate of Ruby's, James Woodard, admitted "funneling" ammunition and dynamite to Cuban exiles.[11] Three, not long after Ruby was jailed for the murder of Oswald, his first lawyer, Tom Howard, asked him if there were any names of people the prosecution could produce that would be damaging to his (Ruby's) defense. Unhesitatingly, Ruby came up with Tom Davis, a known gunrunner to the anti-Castro groups.[12]

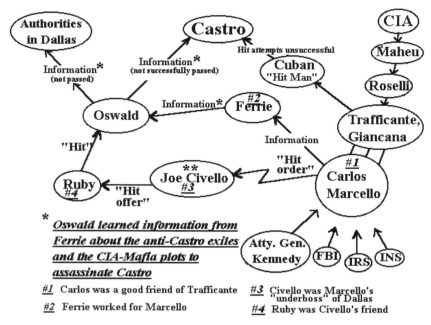

Figure 25: Oswald's connections to the mob

**That Jack Ruby and Joe Civello were friends is well documented. For example, Robert G. Moore's interview with the FBI on November 26, 1963, was consistent with other reports describing a close association between Ruby and Civello. Moore had worked both in a store owned by Civello and as a piano player for Ruby, and testified, "Ruby was a frequent visitor [at Civello's store] and associate of Civello."[13] Also, Ovid Demaris, author of *Jack Ruby*, told the HSCA that he interviewed Civello. "Yeah, I knew Jack," Civello said [according to Demaris]. "We were friends and I used to go to his club."[14] Besides the evidence establishing Ruby's direct ties to Civello, reports of his [Ruby's] friendship with Joe Campisi, the Mob's "number two man" (behind Civello),[15] strongly support the connection between Ruby and Civello. Indeed, George Senator, Ruby's roommate, testified that Joe Campisi "was one of Jack's three closest friends."[16] Moreover, Eva Grant, Jack's sister, acknowledged his closeness to Campisi, saying her brother spent a good deal of time in Campisi's restaurant, the Egyptian Lounge.[17] In addition, the record shows that on November 30, 1963, Joe Campisi visited Ruby in jail.[18] It should also be noted that, considering Campisi's position in the Mob, Marcello could have had either him [Campisi] or Civello contacted to set up the hit on Oswald. Certainly, it could have been either Campisi or Civello (or their associate who recruited Ruby.

had been assassinated, he neither made a deposit nor withdrawal. It really wasn't that strange though, because carrying that much cash around would allow him to legally carry his pistol, which he obviously needed to complete the hit.[19]

Back in New Orleans

While Ruby was trying to take care of business in Dallas, in New Orleans the jury had returned with their verdict and Marcello's trial was back in session. It was 3:00 P.M. Carlos was found "not guilty" on all charges. He was dismissed.[20] Marcello left the courthouse and went directly to his office at the Town and Country Motel. According to sources, Carlos looked "all business" and "as if he had something urgent on his mind."[21] That something urgent was to not give the feds another chance to convict him and to be sure that Ruby successfully completed the hit on Oswald.

Nevertheless Ferrie, even though Carlos seemed to have the situation under control, still felt obligated to help make sure his ex-associate Oswald didn't get a chance to talk. He was going to Dallas just in case he was needed.

Some of what I've presented so far in Part II has been "speculative reconstruction" based on certain facts. I believe, though, that my "reconstruction," if not actually the way it happened, is closer to the truth than any other theories I am aware of. The following chronology, also based on fact or deductive reasoning, further supports my theory (reconstruction).

CHAPTER 9

A Chronology

Friday Afternoon, November 22

1. David Ferrie, shortly after leaving the courthouse at about 3:30 P.M., went to Oswald's former residence on Magazine Street. There, he asked Mrs. Jesse Garner, Oswald's former landlady, if she'd seen the library card Oswald had been using.[1] She declined to speak with him and he became agitated.[2] Logically she assumed he had loaned Oswald his library card and wanted it back. Mrs. Doris Eames, a neighbor, told investigators a similar story.[3] You can be certain that he wasn't concerned in the least about his library card, but surely was hoping that Mrs. Garner would invite him to look for it in Oswald's former apartment. That would allow him to search for any notes or documents Oswald might have left behind about Cuban exiles or plots to assassinate Castro which, if authorities found, could incriminate Marcello, Trafficante, and other powerful individuals as well as severely damage the exiles' efforts. *Of course, Ferrie, probably on the spur of the moment, made up the "innocent sounding" library card story.* He obviously wouldn't have asked her if he could look for anything that had to do with exiles or CIA-Mafia assassination plots!*

---

*Ferrie knew that it was just a matter of time before investigators would be searching the same apartment. First and foremost, Lee Harvey Oswald had his own library card. Card number 8640 was issued to him on May 27, 1963, with an expiration date of May 27, 1966.[4] Evidently, Warren Commission and HSCA investigators "overlooked" this fact or did not connect it with Ferrie's attempted deception of Mrs. Garner and Mrs. Eames, or else they would have probed his suspicious activities further. Second, Ferrie had his own library card (it had

2. Ferrie and two friends, Melvin Coffey and Alvin Beauboeuf, then took off in Ferrie's new light blue Mercury Comet station wagon destined, as they later claimed, for Houston to "do some ice skating." They drove 350 miles through a violent thunderstorm, arriving about 4:00 A.M. on the 23rd at the Alamotel (owned by Marcello) in Houston.[9] I believe they were originally going to Dallas to ensure that Oswald was silenced. It's important to point out that Houston is along one of the preferred routes from New Orleans to Dallas.

3. Meanwhile in Dallas, Ruby had his pistol and seven thousand dollars in cash with him[10] and was beginning to "stalk" Oswald. Ruby showed up at police headquarters about 7:00 P.M.,[11] evidently trying to get a shot at Oswald, who was being interrogated. The fact that Ruby was apparently trying to hit Oswald at the earliest opportunity is consistent with Marcello's order that Oswald be silenced as soon as possible, thereby reducing the chances of his "talking." Ruby didn't get a good opportunity until Sunday morning.

4. A televised news report broadcast either that evening or early the next day alleged that Ferrie was connected to Oswald.[12]

---

expired), producing it later when he was questioned by authorities.[5] Third, it has been noted by researchers that Lee maintained meticulous library dicipline.[6] It would have been important to him to have his own card, not one that was borrowed. Moreover, investigators compiled a long list of library books that Lee borrowed during the summer of 1963.[7] The notion that any of these books were checked out by Oswald with a library card borrowed from Ferrie is frivolous! Fourth, there should be little doubt that Mrs. Garner, if for no other reason than sheer curiosity, looked around in Lee's former apartment (after Ferrie departed) for any library card. The fact that there is no record that she reported finding any library card further supports this author's insistence that Ferrie did not loan his card to Oswald. Fifth, Ferrie's library card, of course, wasn't among Oswald's possessions at the time of his arrest.[8] Finally, if Ferrie was hoping to get Mrs. Garner to invite him to search Oswald's former apartment, he obviously wouldn't have asked her about any items that might incriminate Marcello or Trafficante. Hardly. *Instead, he would have made up an innocous story, such as one about a LIBRARY CARD!* With that said, this author, when referring to Ferrie's visit to Mrs. Garner's rooming house, will simply state the truth, that "Ferrie went to search for incriminating items, etc."

5. Back in New Orleans, it may have been that evening when Mrs. Garner or Mrs. Eames saw that news report. Undoubtedly it prompted them to notify the police about Ferrie's suspicious visit and his implying that he had loaned Oswald his library card. I propose that the New Orleans police took that report from Mrs. Garner (or Eames) as support for that very same news story (Ferrie-Oswald connection). By that time the police and the FBI must have really wanted to question Ferrie about his connection to Oswald and possible involvement in the assassination. They'd have to wait, however, as Ferrie was still in Texas. Logically, while they were waiting they contacted Dallas police to ask if Oswald had Ferrie's library card on him. They must have been somewhat puzzled, though, when told that it wasn't among Oswald's possessions at the time of his arrest. They probably assumed either that Oswald simply wasn't carrying Ferrie's card when he was arrested, or someone in Dallas was trying to cover up any "Ferrie/Oswald" association and confiscated the card from Oswald but didn't list it with his other possessions.

Saturday, November 23

6. In Houston that morning, according to Chuck Rolland, manager of the Winterland ice skating rink, Ferrie did no "ice skating." All he did was make phone calls for about two hours.[13] I believe it was during one of those phone calls that Ferrie received word from Marcello that "things were being taken care of" and he should go back to New Orleans. In fact, according to FBI records, at least one of Ferrie's calls was "collect" back to Marcello's office at the Town and Country Motel.[14] Also, by that time Ferrie may have found out about the televised news report alleging a connection between him and Oswald and his possible involvement in the assassination. It makes good sense that he would have wanted to get back to New Orleans and "defend himself" against those accusations.

7. Perhaps early that afternoon, Wray Gill (Ferrie and Marcello's attorney) found out from his connections "downtown," that, reportedly (from information Mrs. Garner or Mrs. Eames gave to

New Orleans police), Ferrie had loaned his library card to Oswald.

8. About 8:00 P.M., Ferrie and his two friends departed Houston and drove about one hundred miles south to Galveston, arriving about 10:00 P.M.[15]

9. At about 11:00 P.M., a friend of Ruby's, Breck Wall, president of the "mob-infiltrated" American Guild of Variety Artists, also arrived in Galveston, having driven south from Dallas. Then, less than an hour after arriving in Galveston, Wall received a phone call from Ruby.[16] This author believes Ferrie may have met with Wall, and Ruby phoned Wall to confirm the status of the hit on Oswald.

Sunday, November 24

10. At 11:21 A.M., Jack Ruby silenced Oswald. I find it hard to believe that so many investigators and authors are quick to say that Oswald's murder wasn't a Mob "hit." Was it just a coincidence that both Oswald and Ruby had unquestionable links to Carlos Marcello, who had more than sufficient motive* to have Lee silenced? Indeed, it is a matter of record that Ruby's friend

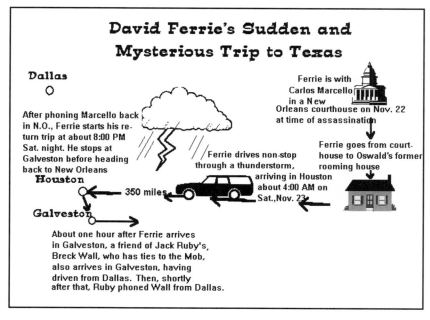

Figure 26: David Ferrie's sudden and mysterious trip to Texas.

Joe Civello was Carlos Marcello's Dallas underboss.[17] Oswald's connections to Marcello are just as certain as Ruby's. In the first place, Lee's mother Marguerite and his surrogate father Dutz Murret were both involved** in Marcello's New Orleans affairs. In addition, as previously discussed, Oswald exploited his long-time acquaintance David Ferrie, who worked for Marcello. If Oswald's, Ruby's, and Marcello's connectivity doesn't make the picture of a Mob hit perceptible, there's more. How can anyone believe that Ruby, who *"just happened"* to have ties to the Mob, *"just happened"* to be wiring twenty-five dollars to one of his dancers who *"just happened"* to be needing cash, from the Western Union office that *"just happened"* to be only a short walk from police headquarters, at *"almost the same exact time" that Oswald was being transferred to the county jail?* You can take it to the bank that Lee's demise was a well-planned, classic Mob hit carried out by Jack Ruby, who was recruited by his friend Joe Civello. This conclusion is not inconsistent with some of Ruby's behavior after his arrest. For instance, while being questioned by the Warren Commission he repeatedly requested that he be allowed to go to Washington, where he'd be "safe" to tell his story. Safe from whom? The best answer is Civello, Carlos Marcello, and their small army of gangsters. Wouldn't anyone, before testifying that they were contracted by the Mob to silence Oswald, want to be in a safe place such as behind bars in our nation's capital? Also, one of the last verbal testaments Ruby made before his death in January, 1967, is suggestive and should be mentioned here: "The only thing I can say is—everything [sic] pertaining to what's happened has never come to the surface. The world will never know the true facts of what occurred—my [sic] motive, in other words. I am the only person in the background to know the truth pertaining to everything relating to my circumstances." At this point the inter-

---

*While Carlos' primary motive was to make sure Lee didn't tell authorities what he knew about the Castro assassination plots, he may well have had other reasons for doing so, and these are are explained in detail at the end of Part II.

** The involvement of Marguerite and Dutz Murret with Marcello and the New Orleans underworld is detailed at the end of Part II.

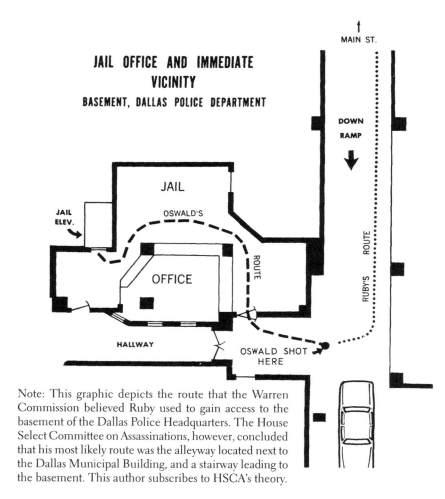

Note: This graphic depicts the route that the Warren Commission believed Ruby used to gain access to the basement of the Dallas Police Headquarters. The House Select Committee on Assassinations, however, concluded that his most likely route was the alleyway located next to the Dallas Municipal Building, and a stairway leading to the basement. This author subscribes to HSCA's theory.

Commission Exhibit No. 2177

Figure 27: Illustration showing jail office and immediate vicinity of the basement, Dallas police headquarters, and the route the Warren Commission believed Ruby used to gain access to the basement. (Author's note included.)

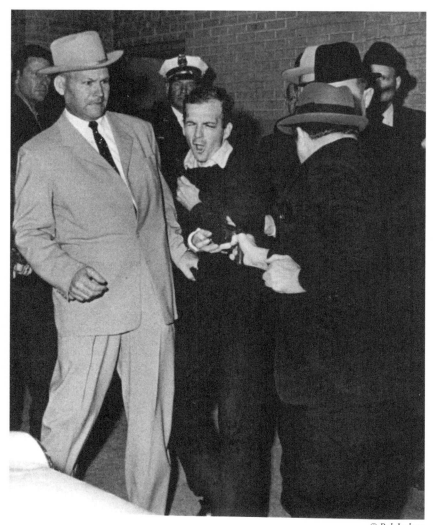

© *Bob Jackson*

Figure 28: Jack Ruby shooting Lee Harvey Oswald

viewer asked Ruby if he thought the truth would ever come out. He replied: "No. Because unfortunately, *these people*, who have so much to gain and have such an ulterior motive to put me in the position I'm in, will never let the true facts come aboveboard to the world."[18]

Ruby makes reference to *"these people."* Considering that he was a friend of Joe Civello, who was Carlos Marcello's "underboss," it may be reasonable to conclude that by *"these people"* he meant the Mob.

Even Gerald Posner who wrote *Case Closed*, in my opinion the "non-conspiracy textbook" on the assassination, said, "The odor of a 'Mafia hit' is all around Ruby's murder of Oswald."[19]

It would be remiss to omit another suggestion of the Mob's involvement in Oswald's murder. Anyone who believes Jack Ruby could get off a shot at Oswald from point blank range, inside the crowded basement of Dallas police headquarters, without "help" from individuals within the department is naive! Organized crime, historically, seems to have been able to get that kind of "help" anytime they needed it.

What's the old saying, "if it looks like a duck, and walks like a duck, it's a duck!" Well, Oswald's murder looked like a Mob "hit" because it was!

11. Early that afternoon Gill went to Ferrie's apartment and told Layton Martens, Ferrie's roommate, "When Oswald was arrested by the Dallas police he was carrying a library card with Ferrie's name on it."[20] Of course, he also told him that authorities wanted to talk to Ferrie about his possible involvement in the assassination.

12. Later that afternoon, from Galveston, Ferrie phoned his roommate. During that conversation there can be little question that Martens told Ferrie what Gill had said about his (Ferrie's) library card being found on Oswald, and that he was a suspect in the assassination. Ferrie immediately departed for Louisiana.[21]

Do you see what must have happened here? It's actually somewhat humorous and, if Ferrie weren't being sought for questioning, he might have laughed when Martens told him about Oswald having his library card. *Ferrie himself created the "rumor" about loaning Oswald his library card when he asked Mrs. Garner if she'd seen the library card Oswald had used, hoping she'd invite him to look for it in Oswald's apartment.* He, of course, had actually wanted to search for any information Oswald might have left behind, mainly about the CIA-Mafia plots to assassinate Castro. New Orleans police, however, receiving their information from Mrs. Garner and Mrs. Eames, actually believed that Ferrie had loaned Oswald his card. The FBI in New Orleans got their information from the police, and a few days later sent a teletype to FBI director J. Edgar Hoover in Washington describing the library card story. The New Orleans police and the FBI were not the only ones who believed Ferrie had really loaned his library card to Oswald. In fact, to this day many investigators, researchers, and authors believe the story and that it somehow supports the idea that Ferrie was involved with Oswald in an assassination conspiracy. For example, conspiracy theorist Mark North (*Act of Treason*) says, and I might add, without any foundation, "Ferrie's library card has been found in Oswald's wallet." Others seem to be puzzled about the entire incident. Indeed, allow me to quote from Anthony Summers', highly acclaimed *Conspiracy* (regarding Ferrie's

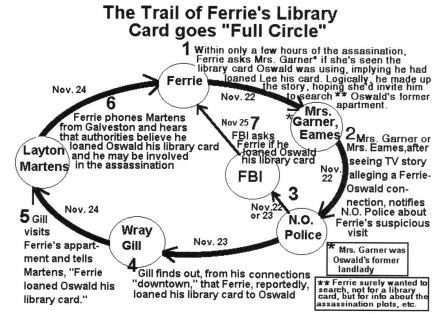

Figure 29: Trail of Ferrie's library card

library card): "This bizarre episode, which may be of key significance, remains unexplained." It's interesting that Gerald Posner (*Case Closed*), who goes into amazing detail about what I think are much less important issues, doesn't even mention the "Ferrie library card" incident. Then there's John Davis' brilliantly done *Mafia Kingfish*. On page 215 Davis writes, "The mystery of David Ferrie's library card has never been cleared up." Guess what readers? After 36 years it's now cleared up! *You now know from reading this what happened to Ferrie's library card...there never was one, at least one that he loaned to Oswald! Ferrie made up the library card story, hoping to be able to search Oswald's former apartment (before the authorities did so) for any information about the exiles and the Castro assassination plots that Lee might have left behind.*

Monday, November 25

13. Ferrie arrived back in New Orleans and was immediately questioned by the FBI. You know what had to be among their first questions. Good guess. They asked him if he had loaned his "library card" to Oswald. Of course he said "no."[22] He later made authorities look a little silly, when he was able to produce his library card.[23] Obviously, Oswald didn't have it, and that's why it wasn't on the list of items Oswald had on his person at the time of his arrest. He also denied ever knowing Oswald.[24] We know that was a lie. Why did he lie? Of course, the answer is because he did not want anyone connecting him to the assassination (which he didn't have anything to do with) or Oswald's murder, which he would have been at least an "accessory" to.

14. For the same reasons, Ferrie lied about why he took off for Texas right after the assassination. At first he told the FBI his trip was "to do a little ice skating and goose hunting."[25] As you recall, the manager of the rink in Houston where they went stated that Ferrie didn't skate and only used the phone for two hours. Then, other witnesses told authorities that he hadn't done any goose hunting. Also, Ferrie said he "wanted to relax after the strain of Marcello's trial." Some relaxation, driving 350 miles nonstop through a tremendous thunderstorm to use the phone for two hours!

CHAPTER 10

The Key Facts

The Powerful, Deadly, Scheming Marcello

1. Marcello, in return for casino rights in Havana (should they be successful in ousting Castro), agreed to help finance the operations of the anti-Castro exiles.[1]

2. From late 1960 until at least* February 1963, high-ranking CIA officials conspired with Mafia figures John Roselli, Sam Giancana, Santos Trafficante, and Carlos Marcello in plots to assassinate Fidel Castro.[2]

3. Marcello in 1979 told undercover FBI agent Joseph Hauser that he was involved in a CIA-Mafia plot to assassinate Castro.[3]

4. Marcello, according to reliable sources, offered one hundred thousand dollars to a Sam Benton in return for his arranging the assassination of Castro.[4]

Oswald Finds Out Too Much

5. Strong evidence exists that Oswald infiltrated the anti-Castro Cuban exiles by exploiting his former CAP commander and recent associate David Ferrie (who worked for Marcello).

6. Numerous witnesses stated that they saw Oswald on several occasions in the office of Guy Banister at 544 Camp Street in New Orleans.[5] That office had been described as the "Grand Cen-

---

*Even though officially, the CIA-Mafia plotting terminated in February 1963, William Harvey, CIA chief of Task Force W (the CIA-Mafia plots were under his direction and control), "ominously" maintained contact with the Mafia until at least 1967.[6]

tral Station" for smuggling arms to the exiles.[7]

7. According to at least one witness, Oswald accompanied Ferrie to an anti-Castro exile training camp in Lacombe, north of New Orleans.[8]

8. Reportedly, while Oswald was in Mexico City he told Soviet and Cuban embassy officials as well as local reporters that he had information about a plot to assassinate Castro.[9]

Marcello and Ferrie Take Action

9. Shortly *AFTER* it was broadcast that Oswald was arrested in Dallas, Ferrie left the company of Marcello and tried to search Oswald's former apartment. He implied to the landlady he had loaned Oswald his library card, asking if she had come across it. Later, when questioned by the FBI however, he was able to produce this card he had supposedly loaned Oswald.[10] Moreover, Oswald had his own library card (Number 8640), issued to him on May 27, 1963, to expire in 1966.

10. Ferrie then, after trying to search Oswald's former apartment, took off heading in the direction of Dallas where Oswald was in custody.[11]

11. Jack Ruby, *a friend of Joe Civello,*[12] was seen by Bill Cox, his bank manager, only three hours after the assassination, carrying seven thousand dollars in cash. The manager said Ruby neither made a deposit to nor withdrawal from his account.[13] Carrying that much cash would make it legal for him to carry his pistol. Later, only about six hours after Oswald was arrested, Ruby was seen at police headquarters where Oswald was being interrogated.[14]

12. *Joe Civello* was Carlos Marcello's "underboss" in Dallas.[15]

13. Ferrie started his return trip to New Orleans after he found out he was being sought for questioning in connection with the assassination.[16]

14. Ferrie arrived in Galveston about one hour before Ruby's friend, Breck Wall, arrived there from Dallas, and a little less than two hours before Ruby made a phone call (Dallas to Galveston) to Wall.

15. Ruby, who said he just happened to be doing business across the street from police headquarters (and carrying his pistol) when

Oswald was being transferred to the county jail, shot Oswald from point blank range in front of dozens of law enforcement personnel.[17]

Telltale Lies

16. Ferrie lied to the FBI about his trip to Texas, saying it was to ice skate and goose hunt. Witnesses stated he neither skated nor hunted. He also said the trip was for "rest and relaxation," but he drove 350 miles at night nonstop through the worst thunderstorm of the year, arriving in Houston at 4:00 A.M. on Saturday. Then, later that day, after using a pay phone for two hours, he departed.[18]

The Theory

I believe the facts strongly support the theory I presented, that *Oswald found out too much* about the wrong guys in New Orleans and was "silenced" for it. He deceived Marcello associates Banister and Ferrie, infiltrated the "Marcello-supported" anti-Castro

---

* While I believe making sure he and Trafficante didn't face charges in connection with the Castro assassination plots was the main reason Marcello had Oswald silenced, there may have been others. Actually, just to say that Carlos had a motive for "hitting" Oswald may be quite an understatement. Certainly this author has strained to be sure that all other possible motives are addressed. There are five others, listed below.

1. It is quite possible if not likely that the Mob (Marcello) was involved in the funneling of arms (mostly from Texas through Banister's office at 544 Camp Street) to the exiles. While the extent of the Mob's involvement is unclear, it probably would have been limited to financing. Nonetheless, if Oswald told the FBI what he knew about Banister's operation at 544 Camp Street, Marcello might well have been vulnerable to federal gun trafficking charges. As you recall, the attorney general and FBI had been seemingly relentless for some time in trying to get any kind of conviction they could against Marcello.

2. As you may also recall, Marcello had been helping fund the anti-Castro exiles' operations in return for them giving him casino rights in Havana if and when they succeeded ousting Castro from Cuba.[19] Carlos originally made his "funding for casino rights" agreement with Sergio Arcacha Smith, head of the Cuban Revolutionary Council (mainly a fund-raising front for the exiles). While Smith was removed as leader in January 1962,[20] there is no evidence that Marcello discontinued funding the exiles. His ambition to control casinos in Havana had not wavered. Unquestionably, for a time at least, Carlos' funding

exiles, and was entrusted with highly sensitive information about the exiles' operations and the CIA-Mafia plots to assassinate Castro. Once in custody Lee's fate was sealed! Carlos Marcello wasn't about to risk losing his empire by giving Oswald a chance to divulge to authorities information they could use to prosecute him or his friend Trafficante. Much too conveniently for Lee's sake, Marcello's Dallas "underboss" Joe Civello, was a friend of someone quite capable and willing to carry out the "hit." That someone was Jack Leon Rubenstein.

---

of the exiles was fully in concert with the government's anti-Castro policy, and there certainly wouldn't have been any thought of prosecuting him for doing so. Indeed, his actions may even have been quietly appreciated by JFK's administration. However, in compliance with his "post-Cuban missile crisis agreement" with Soviet premier Nikita Khrushchev, JFK's policy toward Cuba changed abruptly and dramatically.[21] In March 1963, the president announced a "crackdown" on the anti-Castro exiles.[22] The government showed it was serious on March 31, when the U.S. State Department working with British authorities arrested a group of anti-Castro raiders at an exile training site in the Bahamas.[23] In the months ahead the situation grew worse for those participating in the anti-Castro struggle. On April 5 the U.S. Coast Guard, Customs Service, and FBI began patrolling heavily for exile activity along the coastline and in the Florida Straits.[24] Then on May 1 the government "officially" cut off funding to the Cuban Revolutionary Council.[25] The Kennedys' crackdown on the exiles was unabated. In mid-June the Feds seized an aircraft and explosives in Florida intended to be used in bombing raids against a Shell oil refinery near Havana.[26] One of the worst blows to the exiles though came on July 31. That's when the FBI raided and seized an exile arms cache near Lake Pontchartrain, a little north of New Orleans. Among those arrested were Sam Benton, a Mob figure who often acted as a liaison between the underworld and exiles, Richard Lanchli, a cofounder of the Minutemen[27] (a right-wing paramilitary group), John Koch, a member of the Cuban Student Directorate (a militant anti-Castro organization), and John Noon, a CIA "asset" involved with the anti-Castro program.[28] Moreover, the FBI confiscated a thousand pounds of dynamite along with napalm and bomb casings.[29]

Meanwhile, secretly and undoubtedly illegally, the CIA was still training and funding exiles. What seemed even more peculiar was that Robert Kennedy himself had approved Operation Pinprick, which featured a series of carefully controlled sabotage raids against Cuban economic targets.[30] Was this a classic case of a "do as I say, not as I do" government policy with regard to the anti-

Castro struggle? Evidently though, what it boiled down to was that RFK was not going to put up with any operations whatsoever against Cuba, including some supported by rogue elements of the CIA, that he himself didn't "authorize." Understandably then, Marcello may have believed that if the FBI discovered he was funding these *"unauthorized operations,"* he could be the target of any related investigation. It is not at all inconceivable that, when the news of Oswald's arrest was aired, Ferrie admitted to Carlos that he had told Oswald how he (Marcello) had been helping fund the exiles. If that were the case, Carlos would have had Lee silenced. It's as simple as that!

3. There can be little doubt that Oswald, considering that he evidently visited Banister's office and spent time with Ferrie (some of which, reportedly, was at a Lake Pontchartrain exile training camp), knew detailed information about the exiles' operation. If he divulged this information to authorities in Dallas, the FBI may have inflicted even more damaging if not totally disabling raids against the exiles. For Marcello this would have been unacceptable. His hopes of getting casino rights in Havana were largely dependent on the success of the exiles' struggle, and he would not compromise their chances of success by giving Oswald the opportunity to "run his mouth" to authorities. For reasons of much less importance, just as nonchalantly as one would squash a bug, Marcello would have had Lee silenced.

4. Reportedly while Lee was in New Orleans, he "ran numbers" for Marcello's betting operation.[31] There has been some corroboration of these reports. In 1967, FBI informant Eugene De Laparra testified that Oswald knew Ben Tregle, who ran a "horse book" out of his Marcello-backed bar and restaurant on Airline Highway and subscribed to Marcello's "wire service."[32] Moreover, FBI undercover agent Joe Hauser stated that in 1979 Marcello admitted that Oswald worked in one of his downtown bookmaking establishments called the Felix Oyster House.[33] The notion that Lee ran numbers, though, should come as less than a revelation considering that his uncle and "surrogate" father (Lee's natural father died two months before he was born) Charles "Dutz" Murret[34] was a mid-level bookie in Marcello's betting network for years.[35] Besides that, Oswald's involvement in the numbers game would account for a disparity between his expenses and regular income. More specifically, while his rent was $65.00 a month, and he had a wife and child to support,[36] he made only $1.50 an hour at the Reily Coffee Company.[37] In fact, that disparity grew when on July 19 he was fired from Reily and had to support his family on $33.00 a week he collected in unemployment compensation.[38] There's no question that Lee needed the extra income from his numbers running endeavors. Perhaps then, when Ferrie went to search Oswald's former rooming house he was actually looking for bookmaking related items that could incriminate Marcello, such as a list of Lee's betting clients or even used "betting slips."

It should not be assumed, however, that what Oswald knew about Marcello's criminal activities was limited to his betting network. To begin with, the very bowels of Marcello's underworld operation were entwined throughout the "seedy" French Quarter of New Orleans, where Lee spent a good portion of his short life.[39] Indeed, he was at least familiar with this cancerously corrupt area. His presence there may have been as unobtrusive as a fly around garbage, and being the nephew of one of Marcello's bookmakers ("Dutz"), he was probably quite welcome at any of the French Quarter's countless peccant, Marcello-connected establishments. It is not unlikely that, especially during the time he ran numbers, Lee was "exposed" to Marcello's illegal concerns, including prostitution, loan-sharking, "protection" rackets, slot machines, and even narcotics trafficking. Actually, it would probably be a mistake to characterize the extent of what Oswald knew about Marcello's maze of condemnable enterprises as insignificant.

Also, if Oswald didn't learn enough on his own about Marcello's unlawful activities, he had two other relatively close sources of such information. It makes sense that "Dutz" Murret (as previously mentioned, Lee's uncle and surrogate father) could have written a book with all he knew about Marcello's affairs. After all, he "made book" inside Marcello's mecca of crime for years. Moreover, Dutz was a friend for several years of Sam Saia, well known as a New Orleans crime leader close to Marcello. The Internal Revenue Service once stated that Saia was "one of the most powerful gambling figures in Louisiana."[40] It would be far from unreasonable to say then that uncle Dutz shared at least a few "intriguing" stories with Lee about the villainous goings-on within Marcello's New Orleans domain that he was witness to for so many years while making his less-than-honorable living.

The second "source" was his mother, Marguerite. Allegedly she had lengthy "relationships" with several of Marcello's cronies such as Sam Termine, who was Carlos' chauffeur and bodyguard and much involved in his affairs, and Clem Sehrt, a close business associate of Marcello.[41] Based on her prior relationships there's a good chance she learned "interesting" facts about Marcello's illicit New Orleans practices. While Lee and Marguerite, especially after he joined the Marines, did not spend much time together, no one including Marcello could be certain that she did not share some of this information with him.

Besides everything else Lee might have learned about Marcello's sinful affairs, it would be remiss not to include the Mob "hits" that must have been made on those unfortunate gamblers, narcotics addicts, "protection subscribers" or loan-sharking pigeons who didn't pay up, and others, who Marcello believed threatened his ambitions.

To Carlos Marcello it wouldn't have mattered whether it was "Dutz" Murret, Marguerite Oswald, Sam Termine, Clem Sehrt, Lee Harvey Oswald, or any other individual that he thought knew too much about his illegal activities, if they were in custody for a capital offense, especially the high-profile assassination of JFK, they would have to be "silenced!"

There's an old saying that's a favorite of mine, *"If you f___ with the bull, you get the horns!"* Well, the "bull" was Carlos Marcello, and Oswald did in fact get the "horns," from Jack Ruby,** at 11:21 A.M. on November 24, 1963!

Lee Harvey Oswald was pronounced dead at Parkland Hospital at 1:13 P.M. CST. Ironically, that is where John F. Kennedy had been pronounced dead at nearly the same time two days earlier.

---

5. Finally, Ferrie may have told Oswald about a new CIA plot to assassinate Castro that didn't actually go into full motion until early September 1963. The plot, code-named AM/LASH, was entirely separate from the CIA-Mafia plots. The key figure in AM/LASH was a Cuban, Rolando Cubela, who was an associate of Castro, but because he became disenchanted with the increasing Soviet presence in Cuba offered his services to the CIA. A CIA official, Desmond Fitzgerald, met with Cubela and arranged to supply him with a poison syringe hidden in a fountain pen, which he would use to assassinate Castro. AM/LASH was so secret that even CIA director John McCone didn't know about it. In spite of efforts to keep the plot secret, I suggest that Santos Trafficante (the underworld boss of Florida) found out about AM/LASH from Manuel Artime, a leader of anti-Castro exile operations in Florida and liaison between the CIA and Cubela. I further suggest, considering that Marcello and Trafficante were good friends, that word of AM/LASH was likely to have passed from Trafficante to Marcello, and then to Ferrie (and of course Oswald). While neither Trafficante nor Marcello would have faced charges if Oswald had disclosed AM/LASH to authorities after his arrest, his revelations would surely have blown the lid off the CIA's latest assassination scheme. An aborted AM/LASH plot meant there would be little chance of Castro being removed, and the Mob getting their casinos back. Ergo, to make sure AM/LASH and the Mob's hope of getting their casinos back stayed alive, Oswald had to die.

**Please refer to Appendix I for an explanation of why Jack Ruby would seemingly face profound risks inherent to "hitting" Oswald on behalf of the Mob.

CHAPTER 11

Final Thoughts

If the Mob or any other group had conspired to assassinate JFK, they would have known precisely where Oswald was throughout the assassination and undoubtedly silenced him *before* he left the Texas School Book Depository. Certainly, assassination plotters wouldn't have expected him to make it out of the building, especially considering he had been on the sixth floor and that the entire area was saturated with police. They surely would not have planned to wait until he was in custody and then silence him! The only logical explanation for the events as they actually occurred, is that (as presented in Part I of this work) there was no conspiracy to assassinate JFK!

Clearly, mobsters showed that they were as surprised about the assassination as anyone when they started acting like a swarm of stirred up hornets *after* it was broadcast that Oswald had been arrested. *Within less than an hour of that broadcast*, Marcello and Ferrie parted company. Marcello hastened directly to his office at the Town and Country Motel. The evidentiary value, with regard to this entire case, of what Ferrie did next cannot be overstated! Ferrie went to *search Oswald's former apartment* and then took off *in the direction of Dallas* in a violent thunderstorm. The point here is that, if the Mob (Marcello was "the Mob" in this part of the country and Ferrie his emissary) had been conspiring to assassinate JFK, *they would have searched Oswald's apartment weeks before the assassination and not have scampered to beat the inevitable police search just after he was arrested!* Just as certain as death and taxes, there was "something" Oswald possessed, like a time bomb with the timer activated the moment he was apprehended, that they were suddenly extremely worried about. That "something" was, of course, information, including what he knew, maps, notes, and so on about the exiles and the Castro assassination plots that could incriminate Marcello or Trafficante. The Mob was especially fearful not only because Oswald was in a position to bargain with authorities or trade information for his life, but also because *most of the world was waiting to hear what he had to say!* After Ferrie reached Houston, as FBI records show, he telephoned Marcello. Meanwhile in Dallas, within about three hours after the assassination, Jack Ruby, *an associate of Marcello's underboss, Joe Civello,* had gathered up seven thousand dollars in cash, making it legal for him to carry his pistol. By no later than 8:00 P.M., he had started to stalk Oswald.

The truth is that neither the mob nor anyone else besides Oswald had a clue John F. Kennedy was going to be assassinated on November 22, 1963! But, even though the Mob was caught off guard, and Marcello and Trafficante were, as long as Oswald was in custody, precariously in danger of being exposed, they still reacted in time, silencing the lone assassin!

Epilogue

The Warren Commission, FBI, and CIA

The Warren Commission (WC) received a wide range of criticism for its apparent lack of effectiveness from not only most researchers and authors but also from other official assassination investigative committees and commissions. While I believe much of that criticism is justified, many of the commission's failings were as a result of insufficient investigative thoroughness and cooperation from the FBI and CIA. For example, when the WC requested background information on Lee Harvey Oswald from the CIA, it took several months and follow-up requests just for the CIA to turn over an incomplete file on Oswald. Also, the CIA contemptously witheld from the commission critical information about their collusion with the Mafia to assassinate Fidel Castro.[1] For the WC to investigate all possible "angles" of conspiracy regarding the assassination, information of this nature would have been essential. Other examples of the CIA's sloppy work or deficiency of effort in support of the WC include: (1) providing photographs that were supposed to be of Lee Harvey Oswald at the Soviet embassy in Mexico City, but actually were of someone else; (2) supposedly erasing audio tapes that recorded Oswald talking with embassy officials; and (3) stating they never interviewed Lee Harvey Oswald, when in fact they did exactly that on at least two occasions.[2]

The FBI's investigative efforts and cooperation with the WC were not any better than the CIA's. For example, even though David Ferrie was, as I have proposed in this book, not directly involved in the assassination of JFK, his relationship with Oswald, visit to Oswald's former rooming house and hurried trip to Texas within hours of the assassination, and subsequent lying to authorities about that trip were highly suspicious and should have been more thoroughly checked out by the FBI.[3] Moreover, a complete file on Ferrie should have been turned over to the WC.

Besides Ferrie, FBI investigations of the "suspicious" Guy Banister and Clay Shaw (see Part II for a brief background on Banister) were remiss, and their names do not even appear in the WC report.[4] Additionally, Dallas FBI agent James P. Hosty Jr. neglected to tell Dallas police captain John W. Fritz during Oswald's confinement that only a few months earlier Oswald had visited the Soviet embassy in Mexico City.[5] Also, Hosty did not inform the WC about an angry note that Oswald had hand delivered to the Dallas FBI office only 10 days prior to the assassination.[6]

A possible explanation exists for the apparent sluggish investigative efforts and the FBI and CIA's lack of cooperation with the WC. I believe that both agencies were concerned about the possibility that individuals or rogue elements within their respective agencies might somehow have been involved in the assassination. After all, both agencies had the means and more than enough motive to orchestrate JFK's assassination. Regarding motive, the hatred between FBI director J. Edgar Hoover and both John and Bobby Kennedy is well documented.[7] The FBI's motive, though, was petty compared to the CIA's. Many within the agency were enraged at JFK's reversal of policy that dismantled their efforts to assist the anti-Castro exiles' battle to retake Cuba. Their anger intensified when JFK withheld air cover for the failed Bay of Pigs invasion they so ineptly orchestrated. In addition, the agency was totally opposed to the president's plan to withdraw from Vietnam. Nothing infuriated the CIA more, though, than JFK's firing of their director Allen Dulles and his plan to break up the agency by placing its control under the Department of Defense.[8]

The point is that I believe both the FBI and CIA were reluctant to investigate the assassination so thoroughly that they might uncover evidence implicating members of their own agencies. A phrase by Harold Weisberg (*Oswald in New Orleans*) seems to describe my point rather eloquently, "*Seek (nothing) and ye shall find (nothing).*"

Dereliction?

One aspect of the assassination absolutely infuriates and disgusts me. I'm referring to what I would describe as the dereliction of duty on the part of Dallas FBI agent James P. Hosty Jr. that, I believe, contributed to Oswald's ability to assassinate JFK. Hosty was assigned to "keep an eye on" Oswald while he (Oswald) was in Dallas. While he admits knowing that Oswald had been a defector, was a Communist engaged in Fair Play for Cuba demonstrations, had recently been to the Soviet embassy in Mexico City, and was working at the Texas School Book Depository, *Hosty didn't "think of him at all in connection with the President's trip!"*[9] That would be like learning there is a cobra in your backyard and not doing anything about it. In fact, Hosty was eating lunch when JFK was shot.[10] Hosty was reprimanded by FBI director Hoover for the "slipshod manner in which he handled the Oswald investigation."[11] Subsequently, he was "punished" by being transferred to the FBI office in Kansas City. I find it hard to believe that the same person could have the gall and audacity to profit from speaking engagements, interviews, and book royalties by exploiting the assassination he may well have been able to prevent!

While it is the opinion of this author that "dereliction of duty" accurately characterizes Hosty's handling of Oswald prior to the assassination, the performance of certain Secret Service agents with regard to the assassination should not be assessed less harshly. In the first place, several Secret Service agents on the eve and during the early morning hours of November 22, 1963, consumed intoxicating beverages.[12] Their actions were irresponsible and in direct violation of a Secret Service regulation which states, "the use of intoxicating liquor of any kind, by members of the White House detail, while in travel status, is prohibited."[13] It boggles my mind that this could have been allowed to happen.

Second, I cannot begin to comprehend the dismal response by the Secret Service agents to Oswald's first shot (I shudder at any thought linking that response to the consumption of alcohol by some of the agents). At the moment of the assassination two agents were in the president's limousine, William Greer, the driver, and Roy Kellerman, sitting in the front passenger seat. In the car following the limo were eight more agents (that includes the two that were actually either running alongside or standing on the running boards of that same car). Among those ten agents, when Oswald began shooting, six initially thought they heard firecrackers going off, three immediately recognized the sound as gunfire, and one believed that he heard a motorcycle backfiring. To this author, this team, entrusted to protect the life of perhaps the most important person in the world should have been trained and retrained to precision on how to react to the type of situation that occurred in Dealey Plaza on that unforgettable Friday in 1963. It is inexcusable that those agents didn't react immediately to the sound of Oswald's first shot because they thought it was a "firecracker exploding" or a "motorcycle backfiring!" More than *eight seconds* passed between the first and last shots, enough time for at least one of those agents to shield the president, if not before the second shot, then certainly before the third! The fact that he was left exposed for that long should haunt those agents to their last day.

Each and every Secret Service agent who consumed intoxicating beverages the night prior to the assassination and those ten agents who were either assigned to the president's limousine or the car following the limo should have been fired. To allow individuals such as these who were sworn to protect the president, but did not, to retire from government service and draw a pension for life absolutely appalls me!

JFK, *Reflecting*

I believe that when we reflect on the presidency of JFK, we should not only recall his accomplishments and perhaps his mistakes, but also what he tried to accomplish. In that regard, I don't believe that history has recorded as clearly as it should the fact that JFK actually began the process for the withdrawal of American troops from Vietnam! To be sure, as stated in National Security Action Memorandum No. 263, dated October 11, 1963, JFK approved the withdrawal of one thousand U.S. troops from Vietnam by the end of 1963. Had JFK lived, I strongly believe that fifty-five thousand American servicemen would not have lost their lives in Vietnam, and that is what I'd like to see JFK most remembered for.

Interest in the Assassination

It's my belief that interest in the assassination of JFK will decline steadily over the next 10 to 15 years and then virtually cease to exist. This is because the part of our society that has been so intrigued with and committed to clearing up the unanswered questions about the assassination is comprised mainly of those old enough to have experienced the shock and horror of the assassination at the time it occurred. Sadly, I feel that once that group is no longer well represented amongst active authors, interest in the assassination will all but die out.

Set the Historical Record Straight

Before such a day approaches, I would like to see a panel of the foremost criminal investigators and analysts in the country, after considering all the possible theories and available evidence, chronicle with the best possible degree of certainty the entire assassination of John F. Kennedy and circumstances surrounding the death of Lee Harvey Oswald. I honestly believe that such a chronicle would be highly consistent with with what I have written in these chapters.

> "What was killed was not only the
> president but the promise."
> —James Reston

THE WHITE HOUSE

WASHINGTON

~~TOP SECRET~~ - EYES ONLY   October 11, 1963

NATIONAL SECURITY ACTION MEMORANDUM NO. 263

TO: Secretary of State
             Secretary of Defense
             Chairman of the Joint Chiefs of Staff

SUBJECT: South Vietnam

At a meeting on October 5, 1963, the President considered the
recommendations contained in the report of Secretary McNamara
and General Taylor on their mission to South Vietnam.

The President approved the military recommendations contained
in Section I B (1-3) of the report, but directed that no formal
announcement be made of the implementation of plans to withdraw 1,000 U.S. miltitary personnel by the end of 1963.

After discussion of the remaining recommendations of the report,
the President approved an instruction to Ambassador Lodge which
is set forth in State Department telegram No. 534 to Saigon.

                                        McGeorge Bundy

Copy furnished:
   Director of Central Intelligence
   Administrator, Agency for International Development

                                   cc:
                                      Mr. Bundy ✓
                                      Mr. Forrestal
                                      Mr. Johnson
             ~~TOP SECRET - EYES ONLY~~ NSC Files

            Committee Print of Pentagon Papers
                  BY HS2   7/15/77

Courtesy of John F. Kennedy Library

Figure 30: National Security Action Memorandum No. 263

APPENDIX I

Why Jack Ruby Hit Oswald for the Mob

Jack's Relationship with the Mob

While Jack Ruby was not a member of the Mob per se, his close association with mobsters is well documented and was longstanding. In the 1930s in Chicago, Jack reportedly ran errands for the infamous Al Capone.[1] There is ample evidence that he participated with the Mob in a gunrunning operation to help Fidel Castro overthrow the regime of dictator Fulgencio Batista.[2] In 1959 he allegedly was instrumental in arranging the exodus of Florida underworld leader Santos Trafficante from Cuba.[3] Trafficante had been "detained" by Fidel Castro during the time he was cleansing the U.S. and Sicilian Mob's presence from his country.

Throughout the years, Ruby maintained his association with prominent underworld figures such as Joe Civello,[4] Carlos Marcello's Dallas underboss,[5] and the Campisi brothers, Joe and Sam, who owned the Egyptian Lounge, a restaurant and notorious hangout of Dallas mobsters.[6] It is believed that Joe Campisi was slated to replace Civello as Marcello's Dallas underboss.[7] Moreover, due to the very nature of Jack's business as owner of the Carousel, a Dallas striptease club, he had routine "dealings" with the Mob on a somewhat regular basis.

Jack Ruby, the Man for the Job

I believe there were three primary reasons why the Mob considered Jack to be "the right man" to hit Oswald for them.

One, his relationship with them over the years had fostered the kind of trust they would have had to have in someone who was going to hit Oswald for them. In fact, in an interview with high-profile columnist Jack Anderson, Johnny Roselli, the gangster whose mutilated body was found stuffed in an oil drum floating off the Florida coast in 1976, made a somewhat profound statement about Jack Ruby. Roselli said that "Ruby was the loyal kind of foot soldier" the Mob could call on the spur of the moment to go "blow somebody's brains out."[8]

The second reason was that Jack Ruby had connections deep within the Dallas Police Department[9] that would make the seemingly impossible task of hitting Oswald while he was still in custody an achievable goal.

The third reason was that Jack would have been relatively easy for them to recruit for such a job. Jack was much in need of the kind of cash the Mob would have offered him for his efforts. He owed forty thousand dollars in back taxes[10] and had serious problems at his Carousel club.[11]

A Good Question

While it's understandable why the Mob chose Jack Ruby to hit Oswald for them, it might be less clear why Jack would be willing to do their bidding considering the profound risks inherent in such an evil effort. In the first place, he could easily be shot as he attempted to kill Oswald. Then, even if he were able to "pull it off," he had to know that murder was a capital offense and he would face execution for his deed. Furthermore, Jack was certainly aware that it was not uncommon for the Mob to silence their own hit men not too long after their deadly task had been completed. A case in point was the hit of New York underworld leader, Joseph Columbo in June 1971. A young black man, in front of 65,000 people at an Italian-American Civil Rights League rally in Manhattan, carried out the hit but was himself murdered (case still unsolved) shortly thereafter.[12]

The Best Answers

While there may have been others, I believe the main three reasons why Jack Ruby agreed to hit Oswald for the Mob are as follows:

1. The cash he was sure to receive was the most important reason. It's quite possible that some of the large amount of cash that Jack had in his possession at the time of his arrest was from a down payment for "services due." At any rate, he would not only finally be debt free, but have the money to fix the Carousel or even buy a new club.

2. Jack must have believed that with good representation, even though he'd surely be convicted of some charge related to his killing Oswald,

he would receive a light, "token" sentence.* Jack expected to be regarded as and treated more like a celebrity or national hero than as murderer. In fact, while in custody before his trial, he mistook Secret Service agent Dean Sorrels for an out-of-town newspaper reporter and was beginning to negotiate fees for his story before he realized who Sorrels actually was.[13] Perhaps just as humorously, the next day Ruby asked a court appointed psychiatrist sent to evaluate him for advice on how to handle the book and show business offers he was bound to start receiving.[14]

3. This reason for Ruby accepting the Mob's offer to hit Oswald is more speculative, but hardly inconceivable. As you recall, Jack was involved in smuggling arms out of Texas to various destinations in the Southeast, not excluding the anti-Castro Cuban exiles operating around New Orleans.[15] You may also recall that Oswald had covertly gathered information, mostly from David Ferrie, about those same Cuban exiles including how they were funded and, in all likelihood, where their arms came from. I believe that when Jack Ruby was offered the contract to hit Oswald, he was made aware of the possibility that Oswald might reveal to authorities what he knew about the source of the exiles' arms. Ruby undoubtedly would have realized that such a disclosure might result in the disruption of the arms smuggling operation he was involved in, and, even worse, the steering of any related investigation towards him.

In Conclusion

While not giving much thought to being harshly sentenced, Jack Ruby must have felt that the cash and hero's treatment he was sure to receive for killing Oswald, not to mention the preservation of his arms smuggling operation, were worth facing the risks** that went with the job.

---

*While Ruby was represented by one of the most prestigious trial attorneys of the day, Melvin Belli,[16] he couldn't have been more wrong about his sentence. On March 14, 1964, he was sentenced to die in the electric chair.[17] Ruby's conviction, however, was reversed by the Texas Court of Appeals on October 5, 1966, because of irregularities in the murder trial. Ironically, Jack Ruby died of cancer before his new trial could begin.[18]

**Being shot by those guarding Oswald, or later by the very individuals who hired him to silence Oswald.

Appendix II

A Chronology of the Life of Lee Harvey Oswald

Significant Events in the Life of Lee Harvey Oswald

The author is grateful to Robert J. Groden for his consent to reprint here the following chronology in its entirety from his outstanding book *The Search for Lee Harvey Oswald*.

October 18, 1939	Lee Harvey Oswald is born.
December 26, 1942	Lee is placed in the Evangelical Lutheran Bethlehem Orphan Asylum.
January 29, 1944	Marguerite requests Lee's release from the orphan asylum.
May 1945	Marguerite marries Edwin Ekdahl and the family moves to Ft. Worth.
Fall 1945	Lee starts grammar school in Covington.
January 27, 1947	Lee enters the first grade class at the Lily B. Clayton School in Ft. Worth.
January 1948	The Ekdahls permanently separate.
March 1948	Lee changes to the George Clark Elementary School to continue in the third grade.
September 1949	Lee starts the fourth grade at Ridglea West Elementary School, Ft. Worth.
June 1952	Lee completes the sixth grade at Ridglea.
August 1952	Marguerite and Lee move to New York City. That fall, Lee enrolls in Trinity Evangelical School, NY.
March 19, 1953	Lee is arrested for truancy in New York.
April 16, 1953	At Youth House for Boys, Lee is given a psychological evaluation.
May 7, 1953	Lee is released from Youth House.

January 1954	Marguerite and Lee move to New Orleans. Lee enters the eighth grade at Beauregard Junior High School.
July 1955	Lee joins the Civil Air Patrol.
Fall 1955	Lee enters Warren Easton High and then drops out.
August 1956	Lee and Marguerite move back to Ft. Worth. Lee later enters Arlington Heights High School.
October 24, 1956	Lee joins the Marine Corps after attending high school for only 23 days. He is stationed in San Diego until April 1957.
May 2, 1957	Lee is promoted to private first class and, two days later, is sent to learn aircraft surveillance at Keesler A.F.B. in Biloxi, Mississippi. He receives a clearance of "confidential."
Summer 1957	Lee is stationed in El Toro, California.
September 1957	Lee is shiped to Atsugi Naval Air Station, Japan, to act as a radar operator. Oswald accidently shoots himself.
November 1957	Lee's unit ships out for Subic Bay, Philippines.
March 1958	Oswald's unit returns to Atsugi.
April 11, 1958	For gun possession, Lee receives his first court-martial.
June 27, 1958	Oswald's second court-martial.
September 14, 1958	Lee is stationed on Taiwan for three weeks.
November 2, 1958	Oswald is sent back to the States. Lee takes a one month leave from the Marines.
December 21, 1958	Lee is reassigned to the Marine base in El Toro, California.
February 25, 1959	Lee takes a Russian language proficiency test and applies to Albert Schweitzer College in Switzerland.
March 9, 1959	Lee is promoted to private first class.
March 23, 1959	Oswald receives his High School General Educational Development (GED) Certificate.
August 17, 1959	Lee requests a hardship discharge from the Marines allegedly to help his mother.
September 4, 1959	Lee's early hardship discharge is approved and he applies for a passport.
September 10, 1959	Lee receives his first passport.
September 11, 1959	Lee is discharged from the Marine Corps.
September 20, 1959	On board the SS *Marion Lykes*, Oswald sets sail

	for England.
October 15, 1959	Lee arrives in Moscow and requests Russian citizenship.
October 21, 1959	Lee "attempts suicide" in a Moscow hotel room.
October 31, 1959	Just days after his release from a Moscow hospital, Lee tries to give up his U.S. citizenship at the American embassy.
January 7, 1960	Lee arrives in Minsk, Russia.
May 1, 1960	CIA pilot Francis Gary Powers is shot down in his U-2 spy plane by the Russians.
June 3, 1960	J. Edgar Hoover writes a memo stating that the FBI needs to be cautious about an impostor using Lee's birth certificate and identity.
September 13, 1960	Lee's discharge from the Marine Corps is downgraded to undesirable because of his "defection."
February 1961	Lee writes to the American embassy indicating his desire to return to the United States.
March 4, 1961	Lee meets Marina Prusakova.
April 15, 1961	The three-day Bay of Pigs invasion of Cuba begins.
April 30, 1961	Lee and Marina get married.
February 15, 1962	Marina gives birth to June Lee Oswald.
June 2, 1962	Lee, Marina, and June start the trip to America. They travel by train through Russia, Poland, Germany, and the Netherlands.
June 26, 1962	Lee's first known contact with the FBI. He is contacted by Special Agents John W. Fain and B. Thomas Carter, who meet with Lee in the Ft. Worth FBI office.
August 16, 1962	FBI special agent Fain meets with Lee in the rear seat of Fain's car in front of Lee's home.
October 9, 1962	Lee allegedly rents Dallas post office box #2915
October 12, 1962	Lee starts working for Jaggars-Chiles-Stovall, a photolithography firm.
October 22, 1962	The six-day Cuban missile crisis begins.
January 27, 1963	A. J. Hidell orders a Smith & Wesson .38 revolver.
March 12, 1963	A Mannlicher-Carcano rifle is ordered from Klein's Sporting Goods in Chicago by A. Hidell.
March 31, 1963	Marina takes some photographs of Lee in the backyard of the Neely Street house.
April 6, 1963	Lee is fired from Jaggers-Chiles-Stovall.

April 24, 1963	Oswald departs for New Orleans by bus.
May 9, 1963	Lee is hired by the Reily Coffee Company in New Orleans.
June 4, 1963	One thousand Fair Play for Cuba Committee (FPCC) leaflets are ordered from Jones Printing.
July 19, 1963	Lee is fired from Reily Coffee Company.
August 5, 1963	Lee enters the Casa Roca store in New Orleans and talks with Carlos Bringuier.
August 9, 1963	Lee hands out FPCC handbills and is arrested following a fight with Carlos Bringuier and two of his friends.
August 12, 1963	Oswald appears in court, is found guilty, and fined ten dollars.
August 16, 1963	Lee and three others hand out FPCC leaflets in front of Clay Shaw's Trade Mart. WDSU-TV is tipped off and films the event.
August 17, 1963	Lee appears on Bill Stuckey's radio show "Latin Listening Post."
August 26, 1963	Witnesses claim to observe Lee in Clinton, Louisiana, with both David Ferrie and Clay Shaw.
September 13, 1963	President Kennedy's trip to Texas is announced, but without details.
Late September 1963	Sylvia Odio gets a visit in Dallas from three men. One of them is impersonating Lee Oswald.
September 26, 1963	Lee is supposed to have traveled from Houston, Texas, to Laredo and crossed the Mexican border at Nuevo Laredo.
September 27, 1963	Lee or an impostor arrives at the Hotel Comercio, which is known as a meeting place for *anti*-Castro Cuban exiles, and visits the Cuban consulate in Mexico City.
October 2, 1963	"O. H. Lee" leaves Mexico City for Laredo, Texas.
October 14, 1963	Lee moves to 1026 North Beckley Avenue in Dallas under the name of "O. H. Lee."
October 16, 1963	Lee starts working at the Texas School Book Depository for $1.25 per hour.
October 18, 1963	Lee's 24th birthday.
October 20, 1963	Rachel Oswald, Lee and Marina's second daughter, is born.
November 1, 1963	FBI agent Hosty visits the home of Ruth Paine and Marina writes down his license number.
November 6, 1963	Lee hand-delivers a note to the Dallas FBI office

	just blocks from the book depository. FBI office chief Gordon Shanklin orders agent James Hosty to destroy the note after the assassination.
November 22, 1963	The president is assassinated in Dallas. Oswald is arrested at the Texas Theater and charged with the murder of J. D. Tippit.
November 23, 1963	Lee is charged with the assassination of President Kennedy.
November 24, 1963	Lee Harvey Oswald is murdered by Jack Ruby.

Note: Mr. Groden does not subscribe in any way to the theory that Lee Harvey Oswald was the "lone assassin" of President Kennedy. Conversely, while I respect Mr. Groden's theory, I do not believe it is consistent with the facts.

Appendix III

A Chronology of the Life of Jack Ruby

1911	Jack Rubenstein (Ruby) is born in Chicago. He will live in the city's slums throughout his early childhood.
1915–21	While his father Joseph is frequently arrested for assault and battery and/or disorderly conduct, Jack is a member of a street gang.
Spring 1921	Jack's mother and father separate.
June 6, 1922	Jack is referred to the Institute for Juvenile Research.
July 10, 1922	The institute recommends that Jack be placed in new environment.
1923–28	Jack, now nicknamed Sparky, and his sister, Eileen live in various foster homes. He drops out of high school at age 16, completing the eighth grade. He idolizes former welterweight boxing champion Barry Ross.
1933–36	Jack and several friends leave Chicago and reside first in Los Angeles and then San Francisco. Jack sells betting tip-sheets at San Francisco's Bay Meadows Racetrack. He also sells newspaper subscriptions.
1937	Jack returns to Chicago. He becomes a "street hustler," scalping tickets and buying and selling watches and other small items. His mother is admitted to Elgin State Hospital, a mental institution.
1938–40	He becomes involved with the Scrap Iron and Junk Handler's Union, befriending the union's secretary Leon Cooke and working as an organizer and negotiator.

1941	Ruby and his friend Harry Epstein move to the Northeast, organize the Spartan Novelty Company, and begin selling small cedar chests containing candy and gambling devices known as punchboards.
September 1941	Jack is declared ineligible for the draft.
December 1941	He returns to Chicago and continues his punchboard business through the mail.
1942–43	Jack is emplyed first by the Globe Auto Glass Co., and later by Universal Sales Co.
May 21, 1943	He is reclassified 1-A, fit for active duty. Shortly thereafter he is inducted into the Army Air Force and is assigned to bases in the South.
February 10, 1944	Jack is awarded the Sharpshooters ribbon for his firing of the M1 30 caliber carbine.
Late 1944	He reportedly attacks and beats a sergeant who called him a "Jew bastard."
1944–46	Jack serves honorably. His character and proficiency ratings are excellent.
February 21, 1946	He is honorably discharged and returns to Chicago. He and his three brothers form the Earl Products Co., which sells (once again) small cedar chests. The company also makes small metal items such as key chains, screwdrivers, and bottle openers. He also distributes gambling "punchboards" again.
Late 1947	Jack sells his interest in Earl Products Co. for fourteen thousand dollars. He moves back to Dallas and invests in and helps manage his sister Eva's nightclub, The Singapore Supper Club.
December 30, 1947	Jack changes his name from "Rubenstein" to "Ruby."
1947–52	He meets and becomes friends with Joe Civello, who runs operations in Dallas for the Mob. He continues to manage the Singapore Supper Club, but when business drops off he changes its name to the Silver Spur Club. Nonetheless, business continues to be bad.
July 1952	Financially strapped, Jack sells the Silver Spur to Martin Gimpel and Willie Epstein. He becomes depressed and keeps to himself, hibernating, for three to four weeks in the Cotton Bowl.
Fall 1952	Jack returns to Chicago.
Late 1952	Gimpel and Epstein's Silver Spur club has little business and they sell it back to Jack cheaply. He

	moves back to Dallas.
1953–54	With business improving in the Silver Spur, he obtains interest in and operates the Vegas Club, which features striptease acts. Jack frequents the Egyptian Lounge and meets the owner, Joe Campisi, who is the Mob's number two man (behind Civello) in Dallas. He becomes friends with Campisi.
1955	Jack sells the Silver Spur Club to Roscoe "Rocky" Robinson.
Late 1959	He becomes a partner with Joe Slatin and they open the Soverign Club, described as a plush and expensive nightclub.
1960	Slatin sells his share of the Sovereign Club to Jack, but he once again gets into financial trouble. Desperate, Jack can no longer afford to be the club's sole owner, and sells half of his interest to Ralph Paul. The new partners change the club's name to the Carousel Club and feature a burlesque show.
1960–62	Business at the Carousel is marginal, but Jack continues managing it.
September 1962	He attacks and severely beats the Carousel's handyman, Frank Ferrar.
March 1963	During an argument over wages with one of the club's cigarette girls, he threatens to throw her down the stairs of the Carousel.
June 1963	Jack visits New Orleans, where he obtains the services of a stripper known as Jada.
Fall 1963	The IRS demands that Jack pay six years of back taxes, amounting to nearly $40,000.
November 24, 1963	At 11:21 A.M. (CST), Jack shoots Lee Harvey Oswald in the basement of Dallas Police Headquarters. It is widely believed that one of his police contacts leaves a side door unlocked, allowing him to gain entrance to the basement.
November 30, 1963	Joe Campisi and his wife visit Jack in jail.
February 17, 1964	Jack is convicted of first degree murder and sentenced to die in the electric chair.
October 5, 1966	Due to irregularities in his trial, Jack's conviction is overturned by a Texas court of appeals.
January 3, 1967	Before his new trial can begin, Jack dies of cancer.

Appendix IV

Journal of the American Medical Association (JAMA), a Two-part Article

JFK's Death—the Plain Truth from the MD Who Did the Autopsy*

In Part I, the two former U.S. Navy pathologists, James Joseph Humes, M.D., and "Jay" Thornton Boswell, M.D., who performed the autopsy of President Kennedy on the night of November 22, 1963, speak publicly about this case for the first time.

In Part II, four Dallas physicians, who tried valiantly for 25 minutes at Parkland Hospital to save the life of the president, also break their 29-year silence to recount to JAMA reporter Dennis Breo the facts about that unforgettable and historically important case.

---

*The following article has been extracted in its entirety from the "At Large" column written by Dennis L. Breo in the May 27,1992 issue of the *Journal of the American Medical Association*.

I'm extremely thankful to Sharon Ali and JAMA for their permission to include this two-part article in *Silencing the Lone Assassin*. In this author's opinion, this article represents one of the most important contributions to the historical record on the assassination of President Kennedy.

JFK's Death: Part I

The Plain Truth from the MDs Who Did the Autopsy

There are two and only two physicians who know exactly what happened—and didn't happen—during their autopsy of President John F. Kennedy on the night of November 22, 1963, at the Naval Medical Center in Bethesda, MD. The two, former U.S. Navy pathologists James Joseph Humes, M.D., and "J" Thornton Boswell, M.D., convened last month in a Florida hotel for two days of extraordinary interviews with *JAMA* editor George D. Lundberg, M.D., himself a former military pathologist, and this reporter about the events of that fateful night. It is the only time that Humes and Boswell have publicly discussed their famous case, and it was the result of seven years of efforts by Lundberg to persuade them to do so.

Bullets came from above and behind

The scientific evidence they documented during their autopsy provides irrefutable proof that President Kennedy was struck by only two bullets that came from above and behind from a high-velocity weapon that caused the fatal wounds. This autopsy proof, combined with the bullet and rifle evidence found at the scene of the crime, and the subsequent detailed documentation of a six-month investigation involving the enormous resources of the local, state, and federal law enforcement agencies, proves the 1964 Warren Commission conclusion that Kennedy was killed by a lone assassin, Lee Harvey Oswald.

Humes, who was in charge, calls it "probably the least secret autopsy in the history of the world." It was Humes and Boswell who opened the casket when the President's body was brought by ambulance from

Andrews Air Force Base after the flight from Dallas. It was Humes and Boswell who lifted the former President from his casket and placed him on the examining table to begin a four-hour autopsy. (They were joined later at the autopsy table by Army Lt. Col. Pierre Finck, M.C., who participated as an expert consultant; Finck, who now lives in Switzerland, declined to come to Florida for the joint interview. Humes says he is breaking his 29-year silence "because I am tired of being beaten upon by people who are supremely ignorant of the scientific facts of the President's death."

Coincidentally, on the second day of the interviews, Boswell told the group that a Fort Worth physician, Charles Crenshaw, M.D., had appeared on TV that very morning to argue the claim in his recent book, *JFK: Conspiracy of Silence*, that when he allegedly observed the dead President at Dallas' Parkland Hospital, he was positive that the bullets struck Kennedy from the front, not the back, "as the public has been led to believe." Crenshaw, who was a surgical resident in 1963, is not mentioned in the Warren Commission's 888-page summary report and his 203-page, generously spaced paperback was written with the aid of two assassination-conspiracy buffs. Crenshaw's book is only the latest in a long parade of conspiracy theories purporting to tell how Kennedy was really killed, including the 1991 release of Oliver Stone's film, *JFK*. Humes and Boswell had agreed to the *JAMA* interview without the slightest idea that Crenshaw's book had been published.

Now, his face incredulous with disbelief, Humes exploded with his summation. Pointing toward the window, the exasperated pathologist said, "If a bullet or a BB were fired through that window, it would leave a small hole where it entered and a beveled crater where it exited. That is what "J" and I found when we examined the President's skull. There was a small elliptical entrance wound on the outside of the back of the skull, where the bullet entered, and a beveled larger wound on the inside of the back of the skull where the bullet tore through and exploded out the right side of the head. When we recovered the missing bone fragments and reconstructed this gaping wound where the bullet exited, we found this same pattern — a small wound where the bullet struck the inside of the skull and a beveled larger wound where it exited. This is *always* the pattern of a through-and-through wound of the cranium — the beveling or crater effect appears on the *inside* of the skull at the *entrance* wound and on the *outside* of the skull at the *exit* wound. The crater effect is produced when the bony tissue of the skull turns inside out where the bullet leaves."

'A foolproof finding'

He concludes, "In 1963 we proved at the autopsy table that President Kennedy was struck from above and behind by the fatal shot. The pattern of the entrance and exit wounds in the skull proves it, and if we stayed here until hell freezes over, nothing will change this proof. It happens 100 times out of 100, and I will defend it until I die. This is the essence of our autopsy, and it is supreme ignorance to argue any other scenario. This is a law of physics and it is foolproof—absolutely, unequivocally, and without question. The conspiracy buffs have totally ignored this central scientific fact, and everything else is hogwash. There was no interference with our autopsy, and there was no conspiracy to suppress the findings."

Though the evidence is less well defined, Humes emphasizes that his autopsy found that the other bullet that struck Kennedy, the so-called "magic bullet" that was the first to kill Kennedy and that also hit Texas Gov. John Connally, was also fired from above and behind. He says, "There was an 'abrasion collar' where this bullet entered at the base of the President's neck, and this scorching and splitting of the skin from the heat and scraping generated by the entering bullet is proof that it entered from behind. Unfortunately, at the time of the autopsy, the tracheostomy performed on the President at Dallas in an attempt to save his live obliterated the exit wound through the front of his neck near the Adam's apple. Soft-tissue wounds are much more iffy than bone wounds, but there is no doubt from whence cometh those bullets—from rear to front from a high-velocity rifle."

Still, the other scenarios continue to be painted. "Recently," Humes notes, "there were about 300 people at a convention in Dallas, each hawking a different conspiracy theory about how the President was killed. I think this kind of general idiocy is a tragedy—it almost defies belief—but I guess it is the price we pay for living in a free country. I can only question the motives of those who propound these ridiculous theories for a price and who have turned the President's death into a profit-making industry."

Humes and Boswell had a long, long day 29 years ago, and, in many ways, it has never ended. The 6-foot, 4-inch physically energetic Humes is a commanding presence, and he says, "I was in charge of the autopsy—period. Nobody tried to interfere—make that perfectly clear." The 5-foot, 9-inch, pipe-puffing Boswell is precise and methodical, and he says, "We documented our findings in spades. It's all there in the records. And Jim is not the kind of guy anybody pushes around." Their comments on the record are essential because polls show, in the wake of the film, *JFK* and the glut of conspiracy-theorist authors, that many, if not most Americans disbelieve the Warren Commission finding that Oswald, "acting alone and without assistance," killed Kennedy. To set the record straight, they agreed to relive for *JAMA* their actions of Friday, November 22, 1963.

. . .

On the day the President was shot at 12:30 P.M., while riding in an open motorcade through the sunny streets of Dallas, it was cold and gray in the Washington, DC, area. Commander Humes, then 39, was the director of labs of the Naval Medical School in Bethesda, MD. Commander Boswell, then 41, was chief of pathology at the Naval hospital, which was part of the Bethesda National Naval Medical Center. Humes was Boswell's boss.

Humes had signed on with the U.S. Navy in 1943 to complete his undergraduate work at Villanova University, Villanova, PA, as part of the Navy's V-12 enlistment program. After earning his medical degree at Jefferson Medical College, Philadelphia, in 1948, he completed his internship and residency in anatomic and clinical pathology at the Bethesda Medical Center; the U.S. Naval Hospital in Philadelphia; and the Armed Forces Institute of Pathology in Washington, DC. He was certified by the American Board of Pathology in anatomic and clinical pathology in 1955. His postings included military hospitals in the Canal Zone, Hawaii, and San Diego. He was appointed chief of pathology at the Naval Medical School in 1960 and promoted to director of labs for the medical school in 1961. By 1963, he had performed several autopsies on military personnel killed by gunshot wounds and he had also spent seven years at the Bethesda facility, which he "knew like the back of my hand." Boswell, a graduate of the Ohio State University Medical School, received his certification in anatomic pathology in 1957 and clinical pathology in 1959. He, too, had previously autopsied several gunshot wounds, and most of his military experience was at the Naval hospital in Bethesda.

Ironically, shortly before President Kennedy was shot and pronounced dead at 1:00 P.M. at Dallas' Parkland Hospital, Humes left the medical center to go home. He had promised to help his wife, Ann, prepare for a dinner party for 24 that evening, almost all of them military personnel. Five of the Humeses' seven children were in school, with the youngest two at home. The radio and TV were off, and the couple did not learn of the tragic news until their older children returned on the school bus. He recalls, "The kids told Ann, 'The President's been shot,' and she was telling them, 'That's a terrible thing to say,' when we turned on the TV and learned for ourselves. My wife and I were both very upset, and we decided that a dinner party on this evening was out of the question." Washington phone circuits were jammed, and while Ann Humes tried to get a line to call her guests to cancel, Commander Humes took his son out for a haircut; his first communion was scheduled for the next morning. When father and son returned, they found that Ann Humes had finally found an open phone line, only to have the operator interrupt with an emergency call from the Surgeon General of the Navy, Admiral Edward Kenney. It was 5:15 P.M. and Admiral Kenney said, "Jim, you better hurry over to the hospital."

By the time he arrived at the hospital, Humes was "beginning to get the message that the President's body was en route. There was great commotion and a cordon of Marines and military police." Once inside, he was told by Admiral Kenney, the ranking military officer, "'to be prepared to do an autopsy' on the late President."

'Find the cause of death'

"My orders were to find the cause of death and I was told to get anyone I thought necessary to help do the autopsy, but to limit it to only the help I needed. Hell, I could have called in people from Paris and Rome if I thought it necessary, but as it turned out, I didn't. About this time, I also received a phone call from Dr. Bruce Smith, the deputy director of the Armed Forces Institute of Pathology [AFIP], offering me whatever help I might need. Bruce was a friend and I thanked him, saying I would call later if I needed help."

While Humes had been preparing for his dinner party, Boswell had been at the hospital, going over autopsy slides with pathology residents. He recalls, "Early in the afternoon, we received a call from Dr. Bruce Smith from AFIP, saying, 'The President's body is on its way to Bethesda for an autopsy.' I argued, 'That's stupid. The autopsy should be done at AFIP [which was located five miles away at the Walter Reed Army Medical Center].' After all, the AFIP was the apex of military pathology and, perhaps, world pathology. I was told, 'That's the way it is. Admiral (George) Burkley [the President's personal physician] wants Bethesda.' Apparently, Admiral Burkley had called the AFIP from Air Force One en route from Dallas. Later, I was told that Jackie Kennedy selected Bethesda because her husband had been a Navy man."

Humes was in total charge

By 7:30 P.M., Humes was in his scrubs in the hospital's new morgue, built only four months earlier. He had selected Dr. Boswell as his assistant. The morgue was at the back of the hospital, and, as Dr. Humes stepped *outside* the morgue onto the loading dock, he noticed a crowd milling about and an unknown man carrying a large, old-fashioned "Speed Graphic" camera. Still outside the morgue, the pathologist told the unknown cameraman, "Get out!" Then Humes asked, "Who's in charge here?" The answer was only two feet away, as a man in full military dress answered, "I am. Who wants to know?" Humes explains, "The man who said he was in charge outside the morgue was some general representing the military section of the District of Columbia. I told him what my assignment was and asked him about the chap with the camera. Well, seconds later, this chap with the camera was sent away."

No generals in the morgue

As the general remained *outside* the morgue, Humes stepped back inside to prepare to receive the President's body. He emphasizes, "Nobody made any decision in the morgue except ME. Nobody distracted or influenced me in any way, shape, or form."

Jackie and Bobby Kennedy and a host of others accompanied the motorcade bringing the President's body from Andrews AFB to the Naval Medical Hospital morgue. While Jackie and Bobby Kennedy and the other VIPs were met at the front of the hospital and escorted to upstairs rooms, the casket was brought to the morgue at the rear of the hospital by Admiral Burkley. The bronze casket had one broken handle, and Humes and Boswell opened it. Humes says, "We found the unclothed body of President John F. Kennedy, wrapped in sheets in a swaddling manner, the massive head wound wrapped around and around with gauze and bandages." Together, they lifted the body onto an examining table, and Humes emphasizes, "There was no body bag anywhere near the scene. I cannot imagine how this talk about the President's body being delivered in a body bag got started, but it is absolutely false."

Opening the casket was a "shocking experience" for Humes, who was a Kennedy supporter. He recalls, "His identifying facial features were all intact and there he was, the President of the United States, now dead at age 46 with a terrible wound of the head. He wasn't that much older than me, and other than the head wound, he looked perfectly normal. He was a remarkable human specimen and looked as it he could have lived forever. It was very, very distressing." After the initial shock, however, Humes and Boswell got down to business. Humes notes,

"This is what we trained to do, and we got down to the task at hand."

As Admiral Burkley, the President's personal physician, stood by their side, a team of 10 "locked in" and proceeded to start what would turn out to be a thorough four-hour autopsy. Humes emphasizes, "I was in charge from start to finish and there was no interference—zero. It was myself, 'J' [Boswell], [Dr.] Finck, two Navy enlisted men, who served as autopsy technicians, three radiologists, including chief Jack Ebersole, M.D., and two photographers, including the medical school's chief of photography, John Stringer. He took 14 x-rays of the body from head to toe and we took 52 photos from every possible angle."

He dispels the myth that no photos were allowed. "The medical school's director of photography was a civilian, John Stringer, and, in my opinion, he was one of the best medical photographers in the world. He took 25 black-and-white photos and 27 color photos, all with large 4-by-5-inch negatives. No significant aspect of the autopsy was left unphotographed." He adds, "The wounds were so obvious that there was no need to shave the hair before photographs were taken."

Responding to published reports that photo negatives were seized by the FBI and that the FBI took its own photographs, Humes is incredulous. He says, "Yes, there were FBI and Secret Service people milling about the room. And, at one point, there was an unauthorized Navy corpsman taking photos in the morgue and the FBI quite properly seized and destroyed that film, since the photographer did not have credentials. However, the official photos taken by John Stringer were never touched, and no one from the FBI even had a camera, let alone the intention to take autopsy photos. These reports are an incredible lie."

He dispels another myth—that the morgue was controlled by generals and other brass in uniform. "The President's military aides from the Air Force, Army, and Navy were all present," Humes says, "and they were all in dress uniforms, but they were not generals and their influence on the autopsy was zero. The only high-ranking officer was Admiral Burkley, and he left shortly after the autopsy began to join Jackie and Bobby Kennedy upstairs."

And a third myth—that he was not qualified to do a gunshot autopsy. "I'd done gunshot wounds before and this one was perfectly obvious—there was a huge hole on the right side of the President's head that could only have resulted from the exit of a high-velocity missile. Dr. Bruce Smith [the deputy director of the Armed Forces Institute of Pathology] had initially thought we might want a neuropathologist as a consultant, but once we opened the casket and saw the devastating nature of the president's head wound, we knew that there was no need for the skills of a neuropathologist. I called Dr. Smith back and told him what we had found, and he decided to make available Dr. Pierre A. Finck, who was one of the AFIP's experts in ballistics. I had never before met Dr. Finck, who arrived at about 9:15 P.M."

Finck, a shy, retiring man who had been trained in Europe, was an Army colonel, and he had trouble getting by all the Marines and sailors who were providing security outside the Navy hospital. Once inside, he completed the autopsy team.

Humes emphasizes, "There was a lot of commotion, but we are trained to focus on the task at hand, even under crowded conditions. Bethesda was a large teaching hospital. The morgue room contained an amphitheater which sat 30 to 40 people, and we were used to seeing authorized medical personnel come and go to observe autopsies." Still, he says that the scene in the autopsy room was "somewhat like trying to do delicate neurosurgery in a three-ring circus." The crowd did not influence the autopsy results, Humes says.

Boswell adds, "Sure, there were FBI and Secret Service people observing the autopsy and talking on their radios to people outside the room, and we could hear a play-by-play of what we were doing and talking about, but nobody tried to interfere and we were able to focus on the matter at hand." He adds, "The FBI and Secret Service told us that two fragments of the President's skull had been recovered in Dallas and were being rushed to Bethesda and that bullet fragments had also been recovered in Dallas."

Humes provides a poignant remembrance of the scene. "The people around the President were totally devastated," he says. "There were still in a state of shock and the reality of what had happened had not yet sunk in. Unless you live in Washington, it's hard to imagine the mind-boggling aura that surrounds the President of the United States. These people thought they had let the President down, and now their hero was gone." Boswell adds, "The people who accompanied the President's body to the morgue were the most disturbed and distressed people I have ever seen."

Humes continues, "We were unfazed by all the commotion and concentrated on getting our x-rays, which we read right at the table, and our photographs, which we relied upon for future documentation. 'J' and I both took down autopsy notes and diagrams."

Fatal wound 'blatantly obvious'

The pathologists found two wounds from a high-velocity missile that would later be matched to the military-jacketed bullets fired from above and behind the President by Lee Harvey Oswald. The fatal shot entered the back of the President's skull and exploded away almost a 6-inch section on the right side of his head; the second bullet entered at the base of his neck, but its exit track was not immediately apparent.

"The fatal wound was blatantly obvious," Humes recalls. "The entrance wound was elliptical, 15 millimeters long and 6 millimeters wide, and located 2.5 centimeters to the right and slightly above the external occipital protuberance. The inside of the skull displayed the characteristic beveled appearance. The x-rays disclosed fine dustlike metallic fragments from back to front where the bullet traversed the head before creating an explosive exit wound on the right temporal-parietal area. These fragments were not grossly visible. Two small fragments of bullet were recovered from inside the skull—measuring 3 by 1 millimeters and 7 by 2 millimeters.

"The head was so devastated by the exploding bullet and the gaping jagged stellate wound it created—it blew out 13 centimeters of skull bone and skin—that we did not even have to use a saw to remove the skullcap. We peeled the scalp back, and the calvarium crumbled in my hands from the fracture lines, which went off in all directions. We made an incision high in the spinal cord and removed the brain, which was preserved in formalin. Two-thirds of the right cerebrum had been blown away.

"After the brain was removed, we looked more closely at the wound, and noted that the inside of the rear of the skull bone was absolutely intact and beveled and that there could be no question from whence cometh that bullet—from rear to front. When we received the two missing fragments of the President's skull and were able to piece together two-thirds of the deficit at the right front of the head, we saw the same pattern on the outer table of the skull—a bullet that traveled from rear to front. Every theorist who says the bullet came from the front has ignored this critical irrefutable diagnostic fact. We did everything within the means of reasonable people to record with x-rays and photos what we saw."

The second bullet was more of a puzzle. "If we made a mistake," Humes says, "it was in not calling Dallas before we started the autopsy. Our information from Parkland Hospital in Dallas before we started the autopsy was zero. If only we had seen the President's clothes, tracking the second bullet would have been a piece of cake, but we didn't have the clothes. In hindsight, we could have saved ourselves a lot of trouble if we had known that the doctors at Parkland performed a tracheostomy in an attempt to save the President's life and that this procedure obliterated the exit wound of the bullet that entered at the base of the neck."

'Time to quit speculating'

"The tracheostomy was a gaping wound, about 3 to 4 centimeters around, and we didn't think of it as an exit wound. We also noticed that the Dallas doctors had tried to place chest tubes in the front of the President's chest, but the tubes had not gone in and we found no increase of blood or fluid in the pleural cavity. There was a contusion of the extreme apical portion of the right upper lobe of the lung, but no laceration. We also noted damage to the neck muscles, trachea, and pleura, but there was no bullet. It was bothering me very greatly, like nothing you can imagine, that we could find neither the second bullet nor its exit track. 'J' and I both knew that bullets can do funny things in the body, and we thought it might have been deflected down to the extremities. We x-rayed the entire body, but did not find a bullet." The autopsy was also criticized because the pathologists did not dissect the President's neck to track the second bullet. Humes says bluntly, "Dissecting the neck was totally unnecessary and would have been criminal."

"By midnight, we decided it was time to quit speculating about the second bullet, and I am very comfortable with this decision. It is true that we were influenced by the fact that we knew Jackie Kennedy was waiting upstairs to accompany the body to the White House and that Admiral Burkley wanted us to hurry as much as possible. By midnight, our task was done—it was perfectly obvious what had killed the man. The second bullet was important, but not of overriding importance. We knew we would find the explanation sooner or later."

The explanation came sooner, the next morning at 7:30 when Humes called Dallas to talk to Dr. Malcolm Perry, the surgeon who had performed the tracheostomy. "The light came on when I talked to Dr. Perry," Humes says. "Of course, the bullet had exited through the neck." Referring to Dr. Crenshaw's contention that the wound in the front of the neck was small and round *after the tracheostomy was performed* and at the time the President was placed in a casket, Dr. Humes says, "We found a gaping wound in the front of the neck where the tracheostomy had been performed, and if Dr. Crenshaw was correct, the only possible explanation is that the neck wound was intentionally enlarged while the body was en route from Dallas, and the insinuation of this scenario does not deserve a response."

Humes and Boswell had remained at the morgue until 5:00 that morning, helping to embalm the President's body. Humes says, "We were able to almost perfectly restore the President's appearance, and a local funeral home brought out a beautiful mahogany casket to replace the bronze one from Dallas. When Admiral Burkley and Bobby and

Jackie Kennedy left to take the body to the White House, 'J' and I finally went home." Boswell says, "The mood in Washington was so apprehensive that the commanding officer of the U.S. Naval Medical School, Capt. J. H. 'Smokey' Stover, asked me to drive behind Jim to make sure that he got home safely."

Humes spent most of Saturday, November 23, drafting the autopsy report. In the process, he burned his autopsy notes, but not really. "This is the criticism I keep hearing over and over again," he says, "that I burned my notes and that this means there must have been a conspiracy. Well, it's true that I burned my original notes because they were stained with the President's blood, and I did not want them to become a collector's item, but I burned them *after* I had copied verbatim in my own handwriting the entire contents. I make no apology for this, but I will explain my reason."

"One of my assignments had been to escort foreign Navy officers around U.S. bases. Along the way, we'd always try to show the foreign officers slices of Americana. On one of these trips, we saw an exhibit that purported to be the chair on which President Abraham Lincoln sat when he was shot at Ford's Theater. There were stains on the back of the chair that were reported to be from Lincoln's blood. I was appalled at this type of display, though I later learned that the stains were from macassar, a hair preparation of the day that inspired the antimacassar doily, and not from Lincoln's blood. In any event, when I saw that my own notes were stained with Kennedy's blood, I vowed that this type of revolting object would not fall into the wrong hands. I burned the notes that night in my fireplace."

Admiral Burkley wanted the autopsy report by midnight, Sunday, November 24, and early Sunday morning Humes returned to the Naval medical school to go over his handwritten report with Drs. Boswell and Finck. The three pathologists met in the office of Adm. C. B. Galloway, the commanding officer of the National Naval Medical Center. While talking, they were called to watch a nearby TV set—Jack Ruby had just shot Lee Harvey Oswald in Dallas. Returning to their report, the three experts had no trouble agreeing on the facts of their autopsy. The report, "A63-272," was the 272nd autopsy performed that year at the hospital. The admiral's secretary typed the handwritten report into six pages. Humes says, "Our conclusions have stood the test of time." The cause of death is given as "gunshot, wound, head." The summary, as published in the 1964 Warren Commission report, reads as follows:

The original 1963 autopsy report

"It is our opinion that the deceased died as a result of two perforating gunshot wounds inflicted by high-velocity projectiles fired by a person or persons unknown. The projectiles were fired from a point behind and somewhat above the level of the deceased. The observations and available information do not permit a satisfactory estimate as to the sequence of the two wounds.

"The fatal missile entered the skull above and to the right of the external occipital protuberance. A portion of the projectile traversed the cranial cavity in a posterior-anterior direction (see lateral skull roentgenograms), depositing minute particles along its path. A portion of the projectile made its exit through the parietal bone on the right, carrying with it portions of cerebrum, skull, and scalp. The two wounds of the skull combined with the force of the missile produced extensive fragmentation of the skull, laceration of the superior sagittal sinus, and of the right cerebral hemisphere.

"The other missile entered the right superior posterior thorax above the scapula and traversed the soft tissues of the supra-scapular and supra-clavicular portions of the base of the right side of the neck. This missile produced contusions of the right apical parietal pleura and of the apical portion of the right upper lobe of the lung. The missile contused the strap muscles of the right side of the neck, damaged the trachea, and made its exit through the anterior surface of the neck. As far as can be ascertained, this missile struck no bony structures in its path through the body.

"In addition, it is our opinion that the wound of the skull produced such extensive damage to the brain as to preclude the possibility of the deceased surviving this injury.

"A supplementary report will be submitted following more detailed examinations of the brain and of microscopic sections. However, it is not anticipated that these examinations will materially alter the findings."

That night, Humes hand-delivered the autopsy report, signed by Humes, Boswell, and Finck, to Admiral Burkley at the White House. On December 6, 1963, Humes alone submitted to Burkley his supplementary report, writing in the final summary: "This supplementary report covers in more detail the extensive degree of cerebral trauma in this case. However, neither this portion of the examination nor the microscopic examinations alter the previously submitted report or add significant details to the cause of death."

Shortly afterward, Humes turned over everything from the autopsy to Admiral Burkley—bullet fragments, microscopic slides, paraffin blocks of tissue, undeveloped film, x-rays—and the preserved, unsectioned President's brain. "Burkley said he wanted everything," Humes says, "and he came out to Bethesda to get it. I gave it to him all in one package. What was left at Bethesda? Zero. I didn't make a copy of anything. Frankly, I was glad to be out from under the responsibility. Admiral Burkley gave me a receipt for the autopsy materials, including the brain. It was my understanding that all the autopsy materials, except the brain, would be placed in the National Archives. He told me that the family wanted to inter the brain with the President's body. I don't know what happened to the brain, but I do know that Admiral Burkley was an honorable man."

The medical autopsy of President John F. Kennedy was concluded. The conspiracy autopsies had yet to begin.

. . .

Humes and Boswell concede that Kennedy's body was illegally moved from Dallas, in violation of Texas laws requiring that Texas homicides be autopsied in Texas, and that there would have been less confusion if the autopsy had been performed in Dallas, but Humes emphasizes:

"There was a very, very good reason why this happened. Lyndon Johnson did not know what was going on in Dallas on this day, and for all he knew a cabal could have been in the works. He wanted to get back to his base and his base was Washington, DC. He would not leave without Jackie Kennedy, and she would not leave without her husband's body. Johnson had to get back to Washington, and, ergo, the body had to be brought back. That's that, and I cannot believe that any reasonable person would disagree with this course of action."

He adds, "Several days after the autopsy, I got a call from someone in Dallas demanding that we return the bronze casket that had carried the President's body from Parkland Hospital to Bethesda. I told him I had no idea what had happened to that casket, and I didn't—it wasn't my responsibility. He was very insistent, but so was I."

Autopsy confirmed four times

The autopsy findings have been confirmed many times since 1963, a fact that has been largely ignored in the current hoopla over the film *JFK* and over Dr. Crenshaw's new book and media appearances. The first time was the publication of the Warren Commission report in 1964, and Humes has brought to the interview a copy of his own Warren Commission report signed by Chief Justice Earl Warren. It was only during their interviews with Warren Commission investigators that Humes and Boswell saw for the first time the clothing worn by President Kennedy.

Humes says, "Once we saw the holes in the back of the President's suit jacket and shirt and the nicks on his shirt collar and the knot of his necktie, the path of the second bullet was confirmed. That bullet was traveling very fast and it had to go somewhere. I believe in the single bullet theory that it struck Governor Connally immediately after exiting the President's throat."

Boswell adds, "Having seen the clothing, I now know that I created a terrible problem with my own autopsy drawings. My drawings of the bullet holes on the night of the autopsy did not precisely match up with the actual holes in the clothing, because we were not aware that the President's suit jacket had humped up on his back while he waved at the spectators. These errors were later exploited by the conspiracy crowd to fit their premises and purposes." The clothing was kept in the National Archives, along with the rest of the autopsy materials.

Photos not published

Both Humes and Boswell agreed to the Commission's stipulation that the autopsy photos were not to be viewed. Humes explains, "I agreed with the Commission's decision not to make the photos part of the official report. I had stated in the autopsy, 'The complexity of these fractures and the fragments thus produced tax satisfactory verbal description and are better appreciated in photos and roentgenograms which are prepared,' and I meant it. The head wound was devastating, and if the photos were made part of the Commission report they would have become public. I did not think that these photos should appear on the front pages of newspapers, and I did not trust the ability of the commission to keep them secret. So, "J" and I worked with an artist to reconstruct drawings of the President's wounds, based upon our original measurements. These drawings are very accurate and met the purposes of the Warren Commission. In 1964, there were no crazy conspiracy theories about the death of the President."

It was not until November 1, 1966, that the two pathologists saw the autopsy photos—when they were summoned to the National Archives to help categorize all autopsy materials.

The second confirmation of their autopsy came in 1968, as the result of a request made by Drs. Humes and Boswell themselves. In 1968, there *were* crazy conspiracy theories coming out of the woodwork. On January 26, 1968, Boswell sent a letter to Ramsey Clark, then the U.S. Attorney General, in an attempt to put the issue to rest. The letter read:

"As you are aware, the autopsy findings in the case of the late President John F. Kennedy, including x-rays and photographs, have been the subject of continuing controversy and speculation. Dr. Humes and I, as the pathologists concerned, have felt for some time that an impartial board of experts, including pathologists and radiologists, should examine the available material.

"If such a board were to be nominated in an attempt to resolve many of the allegations concerning the autopsy report, it might wish to question the autopsy participants before more time elapses and memory fades; therefore, it would be my hope that such a board would be convened at an early date. Dr. Humes and I would make ourselves available at the request of such a board.

"I hope that this letter will not be considered presumptuous, but this matter is of great concern to us, and I believe to the country as well."

Four physicians were subsequently appointed to a blue-ribbon panel to evaluate the original autopsy. The four included:

- William H. Carnes, M.D., Professor of Pathology at the University of Utah, Salt Lake City, and a member of Utah's Medical Examiner's Commission. He was nominated by J. E. Wallace Sterling, the president of Stanford University.

- Russell S. Fisher, M.D., Professor of Forensic Pathology at the University of Maryland and Chief Medical Examiner of the State of Maryland. He was nominated by Dr. Oscar B. Hunter, Jr., President of the College of American Pathologists.

- Russell H. Morgan, M.D., Professor of Radiology at The Johns Hopkins University School of Medicine, Baltimore, MD. He was nominated by Dr. Lincoln Gordon, President of The Johns Hopkins University.

- Alan R. Moritz, M.D., Professor of Pathology at Case Western Reserve University, Cleveland, OH, and former Professor of Forensic Medicine at Harvard University, Cambridge, MA. He was nominated by Dr. John A. Hannah, President of Michigan State University.

None of the four had any previous connection with prior investigations or reports on the President's assassination. After an exhaustive study of all relevant materials, the four members of the panel signed and submitted a 16-page report to Attorney General Clark in April 1968, unanimously concluding:

Examination of the clothing and of the photographs and x-rays taken at autopsy reveal that President Kennedy was struck by two bullets fired from above and behind him, one of which traversed the base of the neck on the right side without striking bone and the other of which entered the skull from behind and exploded its right side. The photographs and x-rays discussed herein support the above-quoted portions [the conclusion] of the original Autopsy Report and the above-quoted medical conclusions of the Warren Commission Report.

The panel's report noted, "The possibility that the path of the bullet through the neck might have been more satisfactorily explored by the insertion of a finger or probe was considered. Obviously, the cutaneous wound in the back was too small to permit the insertion of a finger. The insertion of a metal probe would have carried the risk of creating a false passage—in part because of the changed relationship of muscles at the time of autopsy and in part because of the existence of postmortem rigidity. Although the precise path of the bullet could undoubtedly have been demonstrated by complete dissection of the soft tissue between the two cutaneous wounds, there is no reason to believe that the information disclosed thereby would alter significantly the conclusions expressed in this report."

The Garrison prosecution

The next confirmation came in 1969 in New Orleans when Pierre Finck was subpoenaed to testify at the trial of Clay Shaw, as part of District Attorney Jim Garrison's conspiracy prosecution. Shaw, of course, was acquitted, and, until the publication of this interview, Finck's testimony was the only *public* airing of the expert medical opinions on the assassination.

Boswell says, "A careful reading of the entire transcript of Dr. Finck's testimony shows that he held tightly to the facts of our autopsy and supported its conclusions. However, Pierre was a meek and mild man who had been trained abroad, not in the United States. He was very 'brass conscious,' and he thought that generals were out of this world. At Bethesda, Finck was out of his element—an Army colonel in a Navy hospital—and he apparently mistook the President's military aides and other military personnel for generals. During the trial, Garrison was able to exploit Pierre's misperceptions about the scene to give the impression that it was controlled by generals. Jim [Humes] and I state categorically that there was no interference with our autopsy. The patient was extraordinary, the autopsy was ordinary, or at lease as ordinary as it could be under the circumstances."

Boswell knows because he, too, was in New Orleans in 1969 at the request of the U.S. Justice Department. "The Justice Department was so convinced that Garrison was on a fishing expedition in his prosecution of Clay Shaw," Boswell says, "that it summoned me to New Orleans to refute Finck's testimony, if necessary. It turned out that it wasn't necessary." It now appears, Boswell adds, that filmmaker Oliver Stone may have taken Finck's mistaken perceptions about the alleged military presence in the morgue, as detailed in the transcript of the trial, and used it as the sole basis for the mistaken autopsy scenes in his movie *JFK*. Humes calls the movie scenes "absolutely false and ridiculous," but we are getting ahead of the story.

The next confirmation of the President's autopsy came from the 1977 House Select Committee on Assassinations. Congress appointed a panel of nine experts chaired by Forensic Pathologist Michael Baden, M.D., to investigate the medical findings. In his 1989 book, *Unnatural Death: Confessions of a Medical Examiner*, Baden agrees with the findings of Humes-Boswell-Finck but still terms Kennedy's autopsy the "exemplar" of the "bungled autopsy." He writes, "Despite all these errors and for the wrong reasons, Humes came to the right conclusions—that Kennedy had been shot by two bullets from behind, one in the head, and one in the back. They [the wounds] were poorly tracked, but he got the two most important things right."

Humes says he has not read Baden's book and does not intend to. Mindful that this is a rare attack upon an autopsy that was solidly endorsed by an expert panel in 1968, he reacts to this quoted passage by saying, "Imagine that—we got it right, AS DUMB AS WE ARE! What possible purpose can be served by this kind of attack?"

Apprised of Baden's comment, "[Commander Humes] had never done one like it before," Humes incredulously exclaims, "Who had?" As Baden's written criticisms are read to him, Humes indignantly explodes, "False…false…false. My God, where does this stuff come from?" To cite but one example, Baden writes, "He [Humes] also knew that religious Catholics tend to be opposed to autopsies. And he was not in a position to press the issue." Humes replies, "Come on, now. I am a devout Catholic and for 19 years I was Director of Laboratories at St. John Hospital, in Detroit, Michigan, which is a Catholic hospital, with a very active autopsy service. This autopsy was requested by the Kennedy family, who are Catholics."

JFK the film termed a 'hoax'

Then, there is the film *JFK*. Jack Valenti, a former aide to President Lyndon Johnson and the current President of the Motion Picture Association of America, recently described *JFK* as based on the "hallucinatory bleatings of an author named Jim Garrison, a discredited former district attorney in New Orleans." He also calls it a "hoax," a "smear," and "pure fiction," rivaling the Nazi propaganda films of Leni Riefenstahl.

Syndicated columnist George Will says, "*JFK* is cartoon history by Stone, who is 45 going on 89. In his three-hour lie, Stone falsifies so much he may be an intellectual sociopath, indifferent to truth." *New York Times* columnist Anthony Stone says, " Oliver Stone used as his mouthpiece, Jim Garrison, the former New Orleans District Attorney, who in real life bribed witnesses to prosecute an innocent man—and was laughed out of court. Stone alleges a conspiracy among the Army, the CIA, Lyndon Johnson, and countless others—without a shred of evidence." Stone has been quoted as saying his critics are motivated by a "fear of facts." *Chicago Tribune* reporter Paul Galloway responds, "Nope. They were angry with the way he disregarded the facts."

Humes does not disagree with these criticisms of Stone, which he finds mild. His son had recently persuaded him to see *JFK*, and now he tells his colleague, Boswell, "'J', if you see this movie, believe me, you'll need heavy sedation. The autopsy scene bears no relation to reality, the man they have playing me looks older than I am now, and the triangulated shooting scene is preposterously impossible."

Conspiracy fanciers, including Stone, have tried to make much of the fact that the privately owned Zapruder film of the assassination shows Kennedy's head lurching *backward* after being hit. Humes and Boswell have both seen the Zapruder film "30 to 40 times," and they note that studies published two decades ago by surgeon John Lattimer demonstrated that an object struck in the rear by a high-velocity missile similar to the bullets that hit Kennedy *always falls backward* as a result of the jet-propulsion effect created by tissues exploding out the front.

JAMA's Lundberg, a stickler for detail, poses some questions that remain official mysteries:

Who ordered the autopsy?

"It must have been Jackie Kennedy," says Humes. "She made the request through Admiral Burkley." Boswell says, "It must have been Robert Kennedy. He was acting on behalf of the family." Lundberg counters, "Well, we have a lot of 'must haves,' but no answer." Humes says, "Well, George, I hope you're not saying that we shouldn't have done the autopsy! My orders came from Ed Kenney, the Surgeon-General of the Navy. The President's personal physician, Admiral Burkley, was standing beside me at the autopsy table. Jackie Kennedy was waiting upstairs for the body with Robert Kennedy, and what greater authority can you have than the Attorney General of the United States [Robert Kennedy]?" Lundberg concludes, "OK, there were verbal OKs all over the place." Boswell adds, "Captain Stover [the Medical Center's Commanding Officer] was very thorough, and I'm sure he had someone complete the paperwork."

Who made the absolute identity?

Humes chuckles, "Well, the President's face was not exactly unknown. And the body was accompanied by the FBI, the Secret Service, military aides, and Kennedy family members. We saw no need for dental x-rays."

What happened to the brain?

Boswell says, "I believe that it was buried with the body." Humes says, "I don't know, but I do know that I personally handed it over to Admiral Burkley and that he told me that the family intended to bury it with the body. I believe Admiral Burkley."

What was the condition of Kennedy's adrenal glands?

Humes says, "I am not prepared to answer this question now, except to say that the President was *not* 'cushingoid' and did not have the appearance of a man with the odd fat deposits and facial puffiness associated with the cushingoid appearance. As his activities indicate, he was a very healthy and vigorous man. At some time in the near future, 'J' and I will have to sit down and write for history our report on the condition of the President's adrenal glands."

Should the body be exhumed for another autopsy to remove all doubts?

Humes is appalled. "That suggestion is ridiculous on the face of it. There is nothing further to be learned." Boswell adds, "The family would never permit it, anyway."

Boswell concludes, "In hindsight, we might have called in a civilian pathologist like Russell Fisher, who was right next door in Baltimore. We didn't need him to confirm our findings, but it might have removed the doubts, about military control." Humes says, "Russell was a friend and we easily could have asked him to come in to help, but we had no problem in determining the cause of death."

'Irrefutable evidence'

Lundberg says, "I am extremely pleased that, finally, we are able to have published in the peer-reviewed literature the actual findings of what took place at the autopsy table on November 22, 1963. I completely believe that this information, as personally given by Jim [Humes] and 'J' [Boswell], is scientifically sound and, in my judgment, provides irrefutable evidence that President Kennedy was killed by only two bullets that struck him from above and behind and that caused fatal high-velocity wounds."

Humes concludes, "I really have not had much ongoing interest in the autopsy. We did what we had to do in 1963, and we did it right. And, I can't say that the criticism has hurt my career." Indeed, Humes retired from the Navy in 1967 with the rank of Captain; worked 19 years at Detroit's St. John Hospital as Vice President for Medical Affairs and Director of Laboratories; and served from 1986 through 1989 as a Field Inspector for the Accreditation Council for Graduate Medical Education. In 1980, he was awarded the Distinguished Service Award presented jointly by the College of American Pathologists and the American Society of Clinical Pathologist (ASCP). He was President of the ASCP from 1974 to 1975; President of the Michigan Society of Pathologists in 1974; the first President of the American Registry of Pathology from 1976 through 1978; and a member of the AMA House of Delegates from 1978 through 1988. Now semiretired, he is a Clinical Professor of Pathology at the University of Florida School of Medicine, Jacksonville, and lives in nearby Ponte Vedra, Florida where he has his choice of playing 105 golf holes, including the Tournament Players Championship course at Sawgrass. Boswell retired from the Navy in 1965, with the rank of Commander, and worked in Supervisory Pathology positions at Suburban Hospital, Bethesda, Maryland from 1965 through 1972; and with a large pathology group in Fairfax, Virginia from 1972 to 1983. Now retired, he lives in Bethesda.

Humes stops the interview where he started. "The President was killed by a devastating gunshot wound to the head fired from above and behind by a high-velocity rifle. The second bullet that struck him in the back of the neck was also fired from above and behind. That's it. Everything else is adventitious."

It is an apt description. The adventitia, of course, are the external coatings of the blood vessels, giving rise to the adjective, "adventitious," for "added from another source and not inherent or innate…arising or occurring sporadically or in other than the usual location."

It is the perfect description for the growing industry of conspiracy theories from people who are ignorant of the essential facts and yet purport to know how President Kennedy must have been killed, at least in their minds.

JFK's Death: Part II

Dallas MDs Recall Their Memories

Only 90 minutes passed in Dallas from the time Lee Harvey Oswald raised his rifle at 12:30 P.M. until the slain body of President John F. Kennedy was escorted aboard Air Force One for the 1500-mile flight to Andrews Air Force Base in Maryland and the autopsy at the U.S. Naval Medical Center in Bethesda. The medical team at Dallas' Parkland Memorial Hospital spent only 25 frenzied minutes in their futile effort to resuscitate Kennedy, but that whirlwind of events and emotions produced indelible personal memories.

In truth, though, there were no examinations, measurements, or photographs performed in Parkland's Trauma Room 1 that in any way, shape, or form allowed any of the physicians attending the President to make any meaningful evaluation of the entry and exit gunshot wounds, and the forensic circumstances of death. That assignment was left to the autopsy pathologists at the Naval Medical Center, and their comments in the preceding story stand as the definitive version that Kennedy was struck by only two bullets fired from behind and above from a high-velocity rifle.

This is the unanimous appraisal of four Dallas physicians who have broken their 29-year silence to speak with this reporter about their famous 1963 case. Malcolm Perry, M.D., a surgeon, worked the hardest to try to save the patient and performed a tracheostomy in an attempt to create an airway for the dying Kennedy. Jim Carrico, M.D., a first-year surgical resident, was the first physician to treat Kennedy, at 12:35 P.M., and the first to notice the small bubbling wound in the front of the neck that necessitated the tracheostomy. M. T. "Pepper" Jenkins, M.D., the hospital's long-time chief of anesthesiology, rushed to the scene to try to help ventilate the patient. Charles Baxter, M.D., a Surgeon, assisted in the resuscitation attempt. These were the four key players on the Parkland medical team of November 22, 1963.

Previously, the four have kept their memories private, but the agreed to be interviewed by *JAMA* in the wake of a new book written by one of their former Parkland Hospital colleagues, Charles Crenshaw, M.D., that has bolstered conspiracy theorists because of Crenshaw's incredible 1992 claim that the bullets "struck Kennedy from the front" and that the autopsy photos must have been altered, proving "there was something rotten in America in 1963." Crenshaw attributes these statements and others to his alleged intense eyewitness observations of the dying president.

Although the other four Parkland physicians have some doubt about whether Dr. Crenshaw wrote most of the sensationalistic book or deferred to his two co-authors, both of whom are conspiracy theorists, and although they are reluctant to publicly condemn Crenshaw's claims, they emphasize that they believe Crenshaw is wrong.

Since it is hard to prove a negative, no one can say with certainty what some suspect—that Crenshaw was *not even in* the trauma room; none of the four recalls ever seeing him at the scene.

'Dreams of notoriety'

Dr. Perry says, "In 1963, Chuck Crenshaw was a junior resident and he absolutely did not participate in a meaningful way in the attempt to resuscitate the President and in the medical decision-making. I do not remember even seeing him in the room." Dr. Jenkins says, "He may have been in the room, but he was not among the inner circle attending to the patient." Dr. Carrico says, "Charles has extended his conclusions far beyond his direct examinations. Everyone in that room was trying to save a life, not figure out forensics." Baxter adds, "Jim [Carrico] has just made a very astute observation."

Why, then, would Crenshaw make such claims and write a book representing himself as being in the forefront of the resuscitation effort?

Baxter says, "Charles and I grew up in Paris, TX and I've known him since he was three years old. His claims are ridiculous. The only motive I can see is a desire for personal recognition and monetary gain."

Thumbing rapidly through Crenshaw's slender paperback book, Carrico stops at page 16 and quotes Crenshaw's words, "Many of us have dreamed that history's grand scheme will involve us in some far-reaching role or experience, thrusting us into notoriety and dramatically changing our lives." Carrico concludes, "There's your answer, in Charles' own words. I don't have those kind of dreams."

Jenkins says simply, "Crenshaw's conclusions are dead wrong."

Perry concludes, "When I first heard about Crenshaw's claims, I was considering a lawsuit, but after I saw Charles on TV one day all my anger melted. It was so pathetic to see him on TV saying this bogus stuff to reach out for his day in the sun that I ended up feeling sorry for him." He adds, "Crenshaw says that the rest of us are part of a conspiracy of silence and that he withheld his information for 29 years because of a fear his career would be ruined. Well, if he really felt he had valuable information and kept it secret for all those years, I find that despicable."

Crenshaw's book insinuates that the Bethesda autopsy pathologists altered Kennedy's wounds and it specifically charges that "the incision Perry had made in his [Kennedy's] throat at Parkland for the tracheostomy had been enlarged and mangled, as if someone had conducted another procedure. It looked to be the work of a butcher. No doubt, someone had gone to a great deal of trouble to show a different story than we had seen at Parkland."

Well, the physician who did that work at Parkland—Dr. Perry—and three physicians who observed the tracheostomy—Drs. Baxter, Carrico, and Jenkins—all say that the autopsy photos of the throat wound are "very compatible" with what they saw in Parkland Trauma Room 1. Dr. Baxter says, "I was right there and the tracheostomy I observed and the autopsy photos look the same—very compatible." Dr. Carrico says, "I've seen the autopsy photos and they are very compatible to the actual tracheostomy." Dr. Jenkins adds, "They're the same." Dr. Perry concludes, "Of course, tissues sag and stretch after death, but any suggestion that this wound was intentionally enlarged is wrong. When I talked to Commander Humes the morning after the assassination and told him we had done a tracheostomy, he said, "That explains it—the bullet exited through the throat."

Drs. Baxter, Carrico, Jenkins, and Perry emphasize that their experiences in the trauma room do not qualify them to reach conclusions about the direction from which the fatal missiles were fired. In fact, Dr. Jenkins doubts if any of the Parkland physicians even had a good look at the President's head, explaining, "I was standing at the head of the table in at the position the anesthesiologist most often assumes closest to the patient's head. My presence there and the president's great shock of hair and the location of the head wound were such that it was not visible to those standing down each side of the gurney where they were carrying out their resuscitative maneuvers." However, all four agree, in

Carrico's words, that, "Nothing we observed contradicts the autopsy finding that the bullets were fired from above and behind by a high-velocity rifle."

As a result of Crenshaw's medial allegations, the four other Dallas physicians have been besieged with calls from other members of the Parkland medical team that was on the scene on November 22, 1963. Baxter says, "I can assure you that these calls are uniformly in disagreement with Crenshaw's claims. Most of those who know the facts express disgust at Crenshaw's actions and question if he was involved in the care of the President at all. There has not been one call supporting his position."

Crenshaw also claims in his book to have received a telephone call from President Lyndon B. Johnson, asking him to extract a confession from the dying Lee Harvey Oswald. Baxter responds, "Did that happen? Heavens no...imagine that, the President of the United States personally calls for Chuck Crenshaw." Another Crenshaw claim is that he was the last to view President Kennedy's body as he closed the casket and that it was at this point that he observed the head wound. Dr. Jenkins responds, "It is highly unlikely that any physician would have closed that casket."

Carrico emphasizes, "We are trying to save a life, not worrying about entry and exit wounds." Perry says, "The President's pupils were widely dilated, his face was a deep blue, and he was in agonal respiration, with his chin jerking. Jim [Carrico] was having trouble inserting the endotracheal tube because of the wound to the trachea and I didn't even wipe off the blood before doing the 'trach.' I grabbed a knife and made a quick and large incision; it only took two or three minutes." He adds, "So many people have theories about the assassination, but I have yet to meet one who has read the entire 26 volumes of the Warren Commission report."

The continuing controversy over the assassination and the refusal to believe the 26-volume, elephantinely documented Warren Commission report obscure the real human tragedy of the event. Pepper Jenkins recalls one poignant anecdote:

"The President was a bigger man than I recalled from seeing him on TV. He must have had really severe back pain, judging by the size of the back brace we cut off. He was tightly laced into this brace with wide Ace bandages making figure-of-eight loops around his trunk and around his thighs. His feet were sticking off one end of the gurney and his head was at the other end, cradled in my arms. I was standing with the front of my jacket against his head wound, an alignment that put me in the best position to carry out artificial ventilation. I was getting gushes of blood down my jacket and onto my shoes."

"Jacqueline Kennedy was circling the room, walking behind my back. The Secret Service could not keep her out of the room. She looked shell-shocked. As she circled and circled, I noticed that her hands were cupped in front of her, as if she were cradling something. As she passed by, she nudged me with an elbow and handed me what she had been nursing in her hands—a large chunk of her husband's brain tissues. I quickly handed it to a nurse."

"It's too late, Mac"

It was Dr. William Kemp Clark, a Parkland Hospital neurosurgeon, who most closely observed Kennedy's massive head wound. He told Dr. Perry, "It's too late, Mac. There's nothing more to be done." It was Dr. Clark who pronounced the president dead at 1:00 P.M., only 25 minutes after he was wheeled into the emergency room.

By this time, the Secret Service had allowed a Catholic priest to enter the room to administer the Last Rites. Jenkins recalls, "All of the medical staff seemed to disappear, dissolve, fade from the room, except, I believe, for me and Dr. Baxter. I was busy disconnecting the electrocardiographic leads, removing the IV's, and extracting the endotracheal tube. However, before I could finish these duties, Mrs. Kennedy returned to the president's side and I retreated to a corner of the room. She kissed the president on the foot, on the leg, on the thigh, on the abdomen, on the chest, and then, on the face. She still looked drawn, pale, shocked, and remote. I doubt if she remembers any part of this. Then the priest began the Last Rites in deliberate, resonant, and slow tones, and then it was over."

Jenkins recalls that Secret Service agents then "grabbed the president's gurney on each side and wheeled it out of the room, all but running over Dr. Earl Rose, the Dallas medical examiner (whose office was right across the hall from the emergency room)."

Dr. Rose, who is now retired in Iowa City, also gave *JAMA* a rare interview to pick up the narrative. "I was in their way," Rose recalls. "I was face to face with Secret Service agent Roy H. Kellerman, and I was trying to explain to him that Texas law applied in the instant case of the death of the president and that the law required an autopsy to be performed in Texas."

"Agent Kellerman had experienced a tragedy on his watch and, although he had no legal authority, he believed that his primary responsibility was to transport the body back to Washington, DC. He was very distressed, apparently taking the death as a personal affront, and he and

I were not communicating. It was not a hostile discussion, but he and I were expressing differing views on what was appropriate."

A standoff over removing the body

Theron Ward, a Dallas justice of the peace, was at the hospital to assert the applicable Texas law, but, in Rose's words, "he did nothing...he was frozen with fear. In effect, no one was in charge of the situation. Agent Kellerman tried three tactics to have his way—he asserted his identity as representing the Secret Service; he appealed for sympathy to Mrs. Kennedy; and he used body language to attempt to bully, or, should I say, intimidate. I don't recall the exact words, but he and I exchanged firm and emotionally charged words. At no time did I feel I was in physical danger because he and the others were armed. I was not looking at Agent Kellerman's gun, I was looking at his eyes, and they were very intense. His eyes said that he meant to get the President's body back to Washington."

In 1963, Rose was 6-feet, 2-inches tall and solidly built. He was not the kind to back down from a flight if he believed he was right. "I was raised in western South Dakota," he said, "and I carried that baggage with me. People raised in western South Dakota may lose a fight, but they don't get bullied or intimidated." The standoff, however, was soon over. Rose says, "Finally, without saying any more, I simply stood aside. I felt it was unwise to do anything more to accelerate or exacerbate the tension. There was nothing more I could do to keep the body in Dallas. I had no minions, no armies to enforce the will of the medical examiner."

Later that day, Rose autopsied patrolman, J.D. Tippit, who was killed by Oswald; two days later, he autopsied Oswald himself, who was killed by Jack Ruby; a few years later, he autopsied Ruby.

It is 29 years later and Rose, who has a law degree as well as a medical degree, still feels strongly that the Kennedy autopsy should have been performed in Dallas. "The law was broken," Rose says, "and it is very disquieting to me to sacrifice the law as it exists for any individual, including the president. Having one set of rules for the rich and famous and another for the poor is antithetical to justice. There have been many arguments to try to justify the removal of the body, but to me they all seem like retrospective and self-serving theories. People are governed by rules and in a time of crisis, it is even more important to uphold the rules, as this case amply demonstrates.

Rose believes that a Dallas autopsy, which he would have performed, "would have been free of any perceptions of outside influences to compromise the results. After all, if Oswald had lived, his trial would have been held in Texas and a Texas autopsy would have assured a tight chain of custody on all the evidence. In Dallas, we had access to the president's clothing and to the medical team who had treated him, and these are very important considerations."

Further, Rose believes that the removal of the body was the first step in creating disbelief about what had happened. "Silence and concealment are the mother's milk of conspiracy theories," he says. "If we have learned anything in the 29 years since the president was shot, it is that silence and concealment breed theories of conspiracy and the only answer is to open up the records, without self-serving rules of secrecy, and let the American people judge for themselves."

Rose, who is a board certified forensic pathologist and who has personally examined Kennedy's autopsy materials and records, next turned his attention to the claims made by Dr. Crenshaw, who is a surgeon. "I believe that Dr. Crenshaw believes what he is saying when he argues that the shots came from the front," Rose says, "but he is mistaken." Pressed on his degree of confidence in this statement, Rose finally says, "I am absolutely sure that he is in error."

Rose was a member of the 1977 House Select Committee on Assassinations that had access to the entire autopsy file of President Kennedy and that supported the autopsy conclusions. Though he thinks the Bethesda autopsy was "less than optimal," Rose has no argument with the central fact, saying, "I agree that the two wounds to the neck and head came from behind and above and that there is no room for doubt on this finding. The physical evidence corroborates this without question." He concludes, "Do not attribute to conspiracy what can be explained by distrust, inexperience, or ineptitude." Offering his own appraisal of who killed Kennedy, Rose says, "Oswald is the prime suspect and there is no credible evidence for any other suspect. However, there will always be reservations until all the evidence is disclosed. Only this morning the U.S. Justice Department again opposed, on the grounds of national security, a Congressional resolution to open the Kennedy files."

Mistakes and conspiracies

One might think that all this demonstration of facts and expression of expert, medical opinion would end the controversy over the president's autopsy, but one would probably be wrong. Even in that Parkland Hospital trauma room there was one other physician who still disbelieves the president's autopsy report. Robert McClelland, M.D. is a respected surgeon who assisted in the last steps of the tracheostomy on President Kennedy. Interviewed in Dallas, he told this reporter that he maintains a "strong opinion" that the fatal head wound came from the front. Pressed on his reasons, he says, "After I saw the Zapruder film in 1969, I became convinced that the backward lurch of the head had to have come from a shot in the front. Unlike Crenshaw, I do not believe that one can tell the direction from which the bullet came simply by looking at the head wound, as I did, but the wound I observed did appear consistent with a shot from the front. That observation is secondary to my viewing of the Zapruder film, which convinced me that the shots were from the front." Reminded that at least 16 pathologists have also studied the Zapruder film and *also* examined the autopsy clothing, notes, photos, and x-rays and have concluded the opposite, McClelland remains unshaken. "I can't speak for them," he says, "and although I am not an expert in ballistics, pathology, or physics, I still have a strong opinion that the head shot came from the front."

So it goes. McClelland had originally mistakenly written in his hospital chart that the wound to Kennedy's head struck the *left* temple. This error, as published in the Warren report, later prompted a call from the office of New Orleans District Attorney Jim Garrison, who wanted to bring him to New Orleans in 1969 to testify in the conspiracy trial of Clay Shaw. McClelland recalls, "Well, when I told the investigator that I had made a mistake in 1963, there was a sudden silence at the other end of the line."

Mistakes do happen and contribute to conspiracy theories. Similarly, Dr. Jenkins wrote in a 1963 report that Kennedy's "cerebellum" had been blown out, when he meant "cerebrum." Dr. Perry appeared at a riotous press conference on the day of the assassination and said that the fatal shot "might have come" from the front. All have become grist for the rumor mill.

Jenkins was a technical consultant to the making of the film *JFK*, advising on the layout and equipment of the Parkland Hospital trauma room. Assured of director Oliver Stone's passion for authenticity, Jenkins was able to help re-create the 1963 room, right down to the last detail, and also to re-create the original Parkland emergency room entrance, which in subsequent decades has been engulfed by the complex of new buildings constructed at the parent University of Texas Southwestern Medical Center, Dallas. When Jenkins showed up at the set for a day of shooting, he noticed that the actors representing the medical team were all being issued blood-soaked scrub suits. Advising Stone that only he and Mrs. Kennedy were splattered with blood, Jenkins was told by the director, "Oh, doc, people expect to see blood." Jenkins notes, "So much for authenticity." Jenkins himself made a cameo appearance in the film, but says, "I was so bored with the film that I fell asleep and missed my two seconds on camera!"

People expect to read about conspiracy theories and this probably will not change. Earl Rose concludes, "The defamers of the truth can only be confronted and defeated by the truth."

This special report is our attempt to confront the defamers of the truth.
*JAMA.*1992; 267:2794–2803; 2804–07

Appendix V

Overview of the Mock Trial of Lee Harvey Oswald and the Testing by Exponent Failure Analysis Associates, Inc. on the JFK Assassination

The following is a portion of a letter from Dr. Angela Meyer of Exponent Failure Analysis Associates, Inc., to Harold Weisberg, author of *Case Open*. In her letter she provides an overview of the testing done relating to the JFK assassination, as part of *The Mock Trial of Lee Harvey Oswald*, that Exponent FaAA performed in August 1992 for the American Bar Association. This author is thankful to Exponent FaAA, Dr. Meyer, and Harold Weisberg for their permission to reprint this material in *Silencing the Lone Assassin*.

Background to the Investigation

Exponent Failure Analysis Associates, Inc. (Exponent FaAA) is the nation's leading consulting firm dedicated to the investigation, analysis, and prevention of failures of an engineering or scientific nature. Our work is well-known throughout the litigation field and we pride ourselves in utilizing the most state-of-the-art techniques in engineering analysis and demonstrative evidence preparation. This is why we were contacted by the ABA.

In March, 1992, members of the Litigation Section of the ABA approached Exponent FaAA to assist with a Mock Trial presentation for their 1992 Annual Meeting in San Francisco later that year. The ABA asked Exponent FaAA to provide expert witness testimony for both sides of the litigation—a first for our organization. We were also asked to provide all demonstrative evidence (courtboards, video, graphics, and computer animation). After much discussion, the decision was made to put Lee Harvey Oswald on "trial" at the event. Please be advised this was a Mock Trial designed to *educate* attorneys on proper trial techniques as well as the use of technology to display demonstrative evidence. This trial was not used as a forum to prove or disprove that Oswald killed President Kennedy.

Trial Preparation

It was determined that the prosecution would consider the following issues: The Magic or Tumbling Bullet, The Trajectory, Injury Analysis, and Path Trajectory of the bullets. The Defense team, of which I was a member, concerned itself with Ballistics, Other Potential Firing Position/Assassins, as well as "shooting holes" in the Prosecution's case. Both sides utilized the following background information: Warren Commission Report, House Select Committee Report, "Crossfire," as well as a copy of the Zapruder film. In addition, either side could acquire additional materials if necessary, if approved by the other side. That is how we acquired your books. Latimer's medical work was also used extensively and we had many discussions with Larry Howard in Dallas as well.

The Prosecution

The work that the Prosecution team presented you have seen in Posner's book. The lead member of the team was Dr. Robert Piziali, a V.P. and Manager of our Biomechanics Group. Injury analysis was performed using information provided in the record as well as photographs that have appeared in numerous books and articles. The Zapruder film was enhanced and each frame captured as a still to analyze the movements of the vehicle's occupants. During this analysis, the Prosecution was able to detect movement in the lapel flap on Governor Connally's jacket which prompted them to associate this with the timing of the first/second shot. Frame by frame analysis was also used to determine timing sequences for the firings of the three bullets.

Exponent FaAA obtained aerial photographs of Dealey Plaza as well as photographs of each building in the Plaza to assist in the creation of the computer animation of the area. The data was precise, most likely within an accuracy of approximately two inches. Using this information, the potential entry point of the President's head wound, photogrammetric positioning of the Governor and the President as well as reverse projection techniques, the Prosecution located the the positions of the two men in the vehicle and then related the injury positions in the bodies. In this way, the trajectory of the bullet, i. e., the cone that you see in Posner's book, could be estimated. As you can see, there is not a straight line trajectory, but a cone to incorporate the +/- accuracy of the analysis. As the cone happens to take in all of the 6th floor window, the prosecution used this to build a strong case.

The Defense

We were able to maintain a Mannlicher-Carcano rifle and bullets from the same lot that Oswald was alleged to have fired. We concentrated on his ability as a marksman to make that shot: the quality of the weapon utilized, the "better shot" available as the vehicle moved toward the 6th floor on Houston Street, and the timing sequence of shots.

To do this analysis, we instrumented the weapon in all directions so that we could monitor the gunman's head movement as well as the rifle movement when the shots were taken. Dr. McCarthy, our CEO and an expert shot, performed the experiments as well as provided testimony during the trial. We were able to produce timing sequences that corresponded to the sequences found by the House Select Committee investigation as well as Warren Report. In addition, we obtained skulls and attempted to reproduce the "pristine bullet." In one or two instances, a slightly damaged bullet was obtained, in others, it was heavily damaged. Dr. McCarthy also looked at using other weapons, as well as other ammunition, which might have been used to make the shots. We also located positions on the grassy knoll where witnesses alleged to have located the sounds of gunfire. In this way, we developed a "killing zone"—i.e. the first shot was taken from the 6th floor, then the vehicle moves into the "killing zone" location and the other gunmen have better shots. Remember, all we need to do was put "doubt" in the jury's mind with regard to the facts of the case. The Prosecution had the burden of proof.

The Trial

We produced all demonstrative evidence for the trial—graphics of the scene, aerial photographs of Dealey Plaza, video of our tests, and three-dimensional animations of the Tumbling Bullet, Fly-Around Dealey Plaza, Timing Sequence of Shots, Killing Zones, etc. The enclosed tape has a review of the trial. We hope that, as you requested, the tape will be housed in the Hood College library so that students may look at it and gain understanding on how technology can be utilized in the courtrooms of today (and the future).

The trial lasted 16 hours (2 days). It was attended by well over 500 people. We had a real jury, picked from San Francisco residents. The jury, and a shadow jury, were monitored real-time for their responses by jury consulting experts from DecisionQuest. These juries were not able to see their reactions, but the audience was. The trial was presided over by some of the most senior judges in the country, including two Federal Court Judges. Other participants besides Dr. Piziali and Dr. McCarthy were Dr. Cyril Wecht and Dr. Martin Fackler. In addition, actors and members of the Exponent FaAA staff acted as witnesses. The trial resulted in 7/5 split by the jury. 7 to convict and 5 to acquit. I have enclosed a copy of the program from the event for your review of the participants.

After the Mock Trial

We were very pleased with the success of the Mock Trial and the materials that we produced. At present, continuing legal education (CLE) video tape is being produced by our organization for the ABA and its members. Everyone here has their own view of whether or not Oswald was responsible for the death of the President, but Exponent FaAA take no position on this matter. It is my understanding that Mr. Posner contacted Dr. Piziali after he saw the Court TV show. I am not aware of what was discussed, but Mr. Posner apparently thought the prosecution's case was worth discussing and informed Dr. Piziali of such. Thus, Dr. Piziali gave approval for him to utilize their work for his investigation. We were unaware of Mr. Posner's investigation results until we saw the *US News and World Report* article last month (enclosed for your review). I have read the chapter in "Case Closed" which acknowledges the work of Dr. Piziali and his team. It is, however, a bit confusing as to the understanding that the work was done for the ABA and not Mr. Posner.

Since Exponent FaAA has not proved, or disproved anything with regard to the person (or persons) behind the assassination, we have therefore decided to make no public statements with regard to Mr. Posner's book. We leave it up to researchers, like yourself, to analyze all the facts, and myths, and draw conclusions that the rest of us can learn from.

We have been fortunate to have much of our work shown on the national networks because of Mr. Posner's reference to Exponent FaAA. If there is confusion on the part of the media when they request information from us, we correct their confusion with regard to who we performed the work for.

Tests and Analyses on the Assassination Bullet Fragments and Specimens

The FBI's Spectrographic Tests

On November 23, 1963, the FBI conducted spectrographic tests on the majority of the bullet fragments associated with the assassination. A report, dated that same day and signed by Director, J. Edgar Hoover, summarized the results of those tests. The report stated: "The lead metal of [exhibits] Q4 and Q5 [fragments from the President's head], Q9 [fragment(s) from the Governor's wrist], Q14 [three pieces of lead found under the left jump seat in the limousine] and Q15 [scraping from the windshield crack] is similar to the lead of the core of the bullet fragment, Q2 [found on the front seat of the car]."[1] Consistent with that report, Director Hoover in his letter to the Dallas Police Department dated July 8, 1964, stated, "...certain metal fragments...were analyzed spectrographically to determine whether they could be associated with one or more of the lead fragments, and no significant differences were found...."[2]

Critics have insisted that spectrography is an "exact science" and the FBI had the means to conclusively determine whether or not the "bits of metal" recovered from the victims matched the bullet fragments found outside the victims.[3] Therefore, when the FBI didn't report that the bits of metal "matched" the fragments but were only "similar" [or there were "no significant differences"], critics claimed that the metal bits and the fragments must have been parts of different bullets. The implications couldn't have been more clear. There were just too many bullets for one gunman to fire, and the G-men were trying to cover up a conspiracy. Adding to the suspicion, complete results of the FBI's spectrographic tests were not reported to the Warren Commission or made available for the public to review.[4]

The critic's charges, however, are far from being well-founded. In the first place, the science of spectrography *is not as "exact"* as some have suggested, certainly not as precise as neutron activation analysis (NAA).[5] Indeed, often the amount of certain elements within a spectrographically tested sample is recorded in terms such as "a trace," "a slight trace," etc., as opposed to say, "parts-per-million" (PPM).[6] In fact, Howard Roffman, a leading critic and author of *Presumed Guilty*, citing an example of how spectrography was used to prove the innocence of a suspect, stated, *"The former contained a trace of antimony...."*[7]

The point is that, it is not unlikely the FBI's choice of the less-than-definitive term "similar" was made carefully [but perhaps too conservatively] to reflect the accuracy of their spectrographic equipment. Moreover, isn't it conceivable [and really quite understandable] that, because their spectrographic tests failed to "prove," beyond any doubt, that the "metal pieces" from the victims were part of the fragments matched to Oswald's rifle, the FBI chose not to release, even to the Warren Commission, the complete results of their tests? There was nothing sinister about the FBI's spectrographic tests and the manner in which they handled the reports. If they honestly thought the "metal pieces" from the victims were not part of the fragments traced to the Carcano, why on earth would they subject those metal pieces and fragments only a few months later to more precise neutron activation analysis?

The FBI's 1964 Neutron Activation Analysis

In May of 1964, at the Atomic Energy Commission's (AEC) laboratory in Oak Ridge, Tennessee, John Gallagher from the FBI and two members of the AEC staff, working together, performed neutron activation analysis (NAA) on most of the testable fragments and bullet specimens associated with the assassination. Unfortunately, Mr. Gallagher was not an expert in NAA, and while the two AEC staffers were "highly conversant" in NAA, they knew little about forensics.[8] This somewhat unqualified team evidently misread the test data.[9] As a result, in his letter to the Warren Commission dated July 8, 1964, FBI director Hoover stated in essence that the NAA results were "inconclusive."[10] Then, seemingly part of an FBI pattern of not wanting to release evidence they felt wasn't helpful to the investigation, they apparently did not return the little pieces (scraped from the fragments in evidence) they tested.[11] Of course the disappearance of those samples has fueled many additional charges by critics that the government was switching or hiding evidence as part of a conspiracy. Ironically, although the FBI didn't realize it, the results of their NAA tests as interpreted in 1977 by Dr. Guinn,[12] and by Dr. Rahn (to be introduced shortly) in 1996 have been indeed quite helpful to the resolution of this case.

An Important Validation of the FBI's and Dr. Guinn's Neutron Activation Analysis

Abstract

The good news about the neutron activation analyses of bullets and fragments from the JFK assassination.

Kenneth A. Rahn, Sr.
Center for Atmospheric Chemistry Studies
Graduate School of Oceanography
University of Rhode Island
Narragansett, RI 02882-1197

26 August 1996

Prepared for submission to COPA's Third Annual National Conference, 18–20 October 1996, Washington, D.C.

Considering how hard researchers are struggling to better understand the JFK assassination, any piece of good news comes as a welcome surprise. After spending much of the last two years studying the two sets of neutron-activation analyses (NAA) of bullets and fragments from the assassination (done by the FBI in 1964 and the HSCA in 1977), I can now report that a piece of good news is indeed emerging—the fragments appear genuine, both analyses are of high quality and agree closely with each other, and together they provide a simple, straightforward picture in which two Mannlicher-Carcano bullets from one rifle account for every fragment retrieved and analyzed. The joint results also provide strong evidence for two groups of fragments, with members of each group being indistinguishable from each other but the groups being clearly distinguishable. The first group contains the Parkland bullet (CE-399) and Connally's wrist fragments; the second group, the fragments from JFK's brain, the front seat of the limousine, and the rear carpet of the limousine. In the past, the difficult statistical aspects of these data coupled with the variable composition of MC bullet lead have prevented researchers from calculating the all-important probability that the two groups are chemically different. I have found a way to overcome these difficulties and can show that this probability is greater than it might appear at first glance: at least 90% and quite possibly greater than 95%.

Because these analyses have received such bad press for many years (claims of switched fragments, misinterpreted data, etc.), I have paid special attention to these criticisms. I can report that they all seem unfounded, having sprung from incomplete understanding of how NAA actually works. Several of these misunderstandings have been perpetuated for many years by researchers citing other researchers rather than persons familiar with NAA. What do these results mean? In contrast to claims made over the years by various WC supporters, the existence of the first group neither proves the single-bullet theory nor provides strong direct evidence for it. By showing that fragments from Connally's wrist are indistinguishable from the Parkland bullet, this first group provides strong evidence consistent with the SBT but equally consistent with an independent hit to Connally. The second group of fragments effectively ties the head shot and all fragments found in the limousine to the Mannlicher-Carcano. The real importance of the NAA data, however, is the "baseline" picture of the assassination they provide—two bullets, one rifle—that logically must be taken as the operative explanation until stronger evidence is provided for a more complex view.

Kenneth A. Rahn has a B.S. in chemistry from MIT (1962) and a Ph.D. in meteorology from the University of Michigan (1971). For the past 25 years he has worked as an atmospheric chemist both in the U.S. and Europe. During that time his principal analytical tool has been neutron-activation analysis. He has been at the University of Rhode Island since 1973, and is now a tenured full professor at its Center for Atmospheric Chemistry Studies, which he co-founded in 1980. He has been interested in the JFK assassination, particularly its scientific aspects, since 1992.

A Word of Caution from the Author

In recent times, charges that the Mannlicher-Carcano bullets were "not suitable" for Dr. Guinn's 1977 neutron activation analysis (and his tests, therefore, invalid), have been embraced by several leading critics and authors. Believing these charges to be unfounded, this author sought the services of three highly accredited scientists with NAA expertise to objectively and carefully review the charges (along with Dr. Guinn's testimony and full NAA report), and render an opinion as to their merit [if any] and the validity of Dr. Guinn's conclusions. These scientists are listed below. What this author did not realize at the time is that Dr. Rahn had already thoroughly studied and reported on not only Dr. Guinn's work, but the charges of the critics as well.

1. Dr. Kenneth A. Rahn, Professor of Oceanography at the University of Rhode Island–Narragansett and expert in NAA.
2. Dr. Albert J. Frasca, Professor of Physics at Wittenberg University, Springfield, Ohio.
3. Dr. Dean Eckhoff, Department Head and Professor of Nuclear Engineering at Kansas State University, Manhattan.

While Dr. Frasca was critical of some of the techniques used by Dr. Guinn, all three of the scientists were of the opinion that the critic's charges cannot be substantiated. Furthermore, all three scientists agreed with Dr. Guinn's critical conclusion that "among the tested fragments recovered from the limousine and the victims, there was evidence for only two bullets."

With that said, this author strongly suggests that those studying the assassination of President Kennedy give little consideration to the writings and statements of unqualified critics, whose charges against Dr. Guinn and his work are not endorsed by a scientist with NAA expertise and qualifications that are at least equal to his [Dr. Guinn's].

I'm grateful to Doctors Eckhoff, Rahn, and Frasca as well as Mr. Andy Hawk, a student of Dr. Frasca's, for taking significant time away from their regular busy schedule to assist me in this endeavor.

Bibliography

Alan J. Weberman and Michael Canfield, *Coup D' Etat in America*

Anthony Summers, *Conspiracy*

Anthony Summers, *Official and Confidential*

Arthur M. Schlesinger, *Robert Kennedy and His Times*

Bill Sloan, *The Other Assassin*

Bob Callahan, *Who Shot JFK?*

Bonar Menninger, *Mortal Error*

Book of Facts, J.F.K. Assassination (CD-ROM), Macmillan Digital USA

Carl Ogelsby, *The JFK Assassination*

Charles A. Crenshaw, M.D., *JFK Conspiracy of Silence*

Craig I. Zirbel, *The Texas Connection*

Curt Gentry, *J. Edgar Hoover*

David E. Scheim, *Contract on America*

David S. Lifton, *Best Evidence*

Dick Russell, *The Man Who Knew Too Much*

Don DeLillo, *Libra*

Donald Freed and Mark Lane, *Executive Action Encyclopedia of the JFK Assassination*, (CD-ROM), Zane Publishing

Enrique G. Encinosa, *Cuba The Fourth Decade*, March 1997

Frank Ragano and Selwyn Raab, *Mob Lawyer*

Fred Emery, *Watergate*

Gaeton Fonzi, *The Last Investigation*

Gary Wills and Ovid Demaris, *Jack Ruby*

G. Robert Blakey and Richard N. Billings, *Fatal Hour*

G. Robert Blakey and Richard N. Billings, *The Plot to Kill the President*

Gerald Posner, *Case Closed*

Gus Russo, *Live by the Sword*

Harold Weisberg, *Case Open*

Harold Weisberg, *Oswald in New Orleans*

Harrison Edward Livingstone, *High Treason 2*

Harrison Edward Livingstone, *Killing the Truth*

Howard Hunt, *Give Us This Day*

HSCA Report and 12 Volumes of *Hearings Before the President's Commission*....

Hugh C. McDonald, *Appointment in Dallas*

I. MacSiccar, *John F. Kennedy*

James P. Hosty Jr., *Assignment: Oswald*

James R. Duffy, *Conspiracy*

Jay Epstein, *Inquest*

Jerry Bruno and Jeff Greenfield, *The Advance Man*

Jim Bishop, *The Day Kennedy Was Shot*

Jim Marrs, *Crossfire*

Jim Moore, *Conspiracy of One*

John Connally, *In History's Shadow*

John H. Davis, *Mafia Kingfish*

John Newman, *Oswald and the CIA*

John Prados, *President's Secret Wars*

Journal of the American Medical Association (JAMA), May 27, 1992

Kenneth P. O'Donnell and David Powers, *"Johnny, We Hardly Knew Ye"*

La Fontaine, *Oswald Talked*

Lester David and Irene David, *Bobby Kennedy*

Mark Lane, *Plausible Denial*

Mark Lane, *Rush to Judgment*

Mark North, *Act of Treason*

Michael Benson, *Who's Who in the JFK Assassination*

Michael L. Kurtz, *Crime of the Century*

National Archives, Depository at College Park, Maryland

Norman Mailer, *Oswald's Tale*

Oleg Nechiporenko, *Passport to Assassination*

PBS Documentary, *Frontline*, November 16, 1996, Failure Analysis Assoc., Inc.

Peter Dale Scott, *Deep Politics and the Death of JFK*

Priscilla Johnson McMillan, *Marina and Lee*

Robert J. Groden, *The Killing of a President*

Robert J. Groden, *The Search For Lee Harvey Oswald*

Robert J. Groden and Harrison Edward Livingstone, *High Treason*

Robert Maheu and Richard Hack, *Next to Hughes*

Robert D. Morrow, *Betrayal*

Ronald Goldfarb, *Perfect Villains, Imperfect Heroes*
Rosemary James and Jack Wardlaw, *Plot or Politics?*
Sam and Chuck Giancana, *Double Cross*
Seth Kantor, *The Ruby Cover-Up*
Sybil Leek and Burt R. Sugar, *The Assassination Chain*
Sylvia Meagher, *Accessories After the Fact*
Thomas G. Buchanan, *Who Killed Kennedy?*
Walt Brown, *Treachery in Dallas*
Walt Brown, *The People v. Lee Harvey Oswald*
Warren Commission Report and 26 Volumes of *Hearings and Exhibits*
Warren Hinckle and William Turner, *Deadly Secrets*
William Manchester, *The Death of a President*

References

Preface

1 J.E. Treherne, *The Strange History of Bonnie and Clyde*, p. 202.

2 Robert J. Groden, *The Killing of a President*, p. 200

3 Gerald Posner, *Case Closed*, p. 253

4 Warren Commission Report (WCR), p. 85; House Select Committee on Assassinations (HSCA), vol I, pp. 566-567

PART 1, *LEE, THE LONE ASSASSIN*
Chapter 1, *The Gunman or Gunmen?*

1 WCR, pp. 105-109

2 Jim Garrison, *On the Trail of the Assassins*, p. 281

3 Ibid, p. 282

4 Ibid., p. 281

5 Gerald Posner, *Case Closed*, p. 304

6 Ibid.

7 Ibid., p. 338

8 Ibid.

9 WCR, pp. 106-107

10 HSCA, Report, p. 82

11 Jim Moore, *Conspiracy of One*, p. 170

12 Gerald Posner, *Case Closed*, p. 327

13 Ibid., p. 328; HSCA, Report, p. 46

14 Gerald Posner, *Case Closed*, p. 328

15 HSCA, Report, p. 46

16 Gerald Posner, *Case Closed*, p. 329

17 WCR, p. 85

18 Gerald Posner, *Case Closed*, p. 342

19 *The Journal of the American Medical Association*, May 27, 1992, "JFK's Death"

20 Warren Commission Hearings (WCH), vol II, pp. 376-384

21 WCR, p. 85; HSCA, vol I, pp. 566-567

22 *Case Closed*, p. 342; HSCA, Report, p. 45; Anthony Summers, *Conspiracy*, pp. 33-34

23 HSCA, vol I, p. 496-504

24 Ibid.

25 WCR, p. 85

26 Gerald Posner, *Case Closed*, p. 315

27 Ibid., p. 316

28 Ibid.

29 Ibid., p. 318

30 Ibid.

31 WC, vol IV, pp. 132-133

32 Gerald Posner, *Case Closed*, p. 322

33 Ibid., p. 324

34 Ibid., p. 325

35 Ibid., p. 324

36 Harold Weisberg, *Case Open*, p. 30

37 Gerald Posner, *Case Closed*, p. 321

38 Harold Weisberg, *Case Open*, p. 30

39 Gerald Posner, *Case Closed*, p. 322

40 WCR, p. 85; HSCA, vol I, pp. 566-567

41 PBS Documentary, *Frontline*, Nov. 16, 1996, Failure Analysis Assoc., Inc.

Chapter 2, *Meet Lee Harvey Oswald*

1 WCR, pp. 143-144

2 Ibid., p. 71, Gerald Posner, *Case Closed*, p. 242

3 WCR, p. 140

4 Ibid., p. 79

5 Ibid., p. 145

6 WCH, vol III, p. 148

7 WCR, p. 143

8 Ibid., p. 141

9 Ibid., p. 143

10 Ibid., p. 125

11 Ibid.

12 WCR, p. 127

13 Jim Moore, *Conspiracy of One*, p. 210

14 WCR, p. 127

15 Gerald Posner, *Case Closed*, p. 283

16 PBS documentary, *Frontline*, Nov. 16, 1996

17 Thomas G. Buchanan, *Who Killed Kennedy?*, p. 106

18 WCR, p. 118

19 Ibid., p. 119

20 Ibid., p. 122

21 Ibid.

22 Ibid., p. 121

23 Ibid., p. 122

24 Ibid., p. 181

25 Ibid., p. 119

26 Ibid., p. 118

27 Ibid., p. 130

28 Ibid.

29 Ibid., pp. 131-133

30 Gerald Posner, *Case Closed*, p. 223

31 WCR, p. 134

32 Ibid., p. 135

33 Ibid., p. 136

34 Ibid., p. 131

35 Ibid., p. 86

36 Ibid., p. 85

37 HSCA, vol I, pp. 566-567

38 WCR, p. 85

39 Jim Garrison, *On the Trail of the Assassins*, p. 281

40 WCR, p. 85

41 Ibid., p. 156

42 Ibid., pp. 157-159

43 Gerald Posner, *Case Closed*, p. 201

44 WCR, p. 157

45 Ibid., p. 159

46 Ibid., pp. 161-162

47 Robert J. Groden, *The Killing of a President*, p. 94

48 WCR, p. 163

49 Ibid.

50 Ibid., p. 166

51 Ibid., p. 165

52 Ibid., p. 168

53 Ibid., p. 171

54 Ibid.

55 WCH, vol XVII, p. 264 (CE-592)

56 WCR, p. 172

57 Ibid., p. 174

58 Ibid.

59 Ibid., p. 178

60 Ibid.

61 Ibid.

62 Ibid.

63 Ibid., pp. 163-165

64 Ibid., p. 175

65 Ibid., p. 180

66 Ibid., pp. 561-562

67 Ibid., p. 180

68 Ibid., p. 181

69 Ibid.

70 Ibid., p. 182

71 Ibid., p. 15

72 Ibid., p. 182

73 Ibid.

74 Ibid.

75 Jim Moore, *Conspiracy of One*, p. 190

76 WCR, p. 195

77 Ibid., p. 185

78 Ibid.

79 Ibid.

80 G. Robert Blakey and Richard N. Billings, *Fatal Hour*, p. 384

81 Ibid., p. 385

82 WCR, p. 186

83 HSCA, vol I, p. 502

Chapter 3, *No Conspiracy*

1 WCR, pp. 730-731

2 Ibid. p. 733

3 Ibid., p. 734

4 Ibid., p. 734-736

5 Ibid., p. 736

6 Ibid., p. 730

7 Ibid.

8 Ibid.

9 Ibid., p. 731

10 Ibid.

11 Ibid., pp. 731-732

12 Ibid., p. 732

13 *The Fourth Decade*, March, 1997, p. 11

14 WCR, p. 733

15 Ibid., p. 734

16 James P. Hosty, Jr., *Assignment: Oswald*, p. 214

17 Ibid., p. 217

18 WCH, vol XXV, p. 823 (CE-2570)

19 WCR, p. 735

20 Ibid.

21 Ibid.

22 Ibid.

23 Ibid.

Chapter 4, *Not an Act*

1 Gerald Posner, *Case Closed*, p. 16

2 Ibid., p. 51

3 Ibid., p. 115

4 PBS Documentry, *Frontline*, Nov. 16, 1996

5 Gerald Posner, *Case Closed*, p. 163

6 Norman Mailer, *Oswald's Tale*, p. 598

7 PBS documentry, *Frontline*, Nov. 16, 1996, *Who Was Lee Harvey Oswald?*

8 Ibid.

9 Oleg Nechiporenko, *Passport to Assassination*, p. 77

Chapter 5, *Points of No Conspiracy*

1 Gerald Posner, *Case Closed*, p. 169

2 Norman Mailer, *Oswald's Tale*, p. 600

3 Gerald Posner, *Case Closed*, p. 113

4 Ibid., p. 114

5 Ibid., p. 197

6 WCR, p. 246

7 Gerald Posner, *Case Closed*, p. 202

8 Ibid., p. 198

9 Ibid., p. 211

10 Ibid.

11 Ibid., p. 218

12 *The Fourth Decade*, vol 4, No. 3, p. 16

13 Ibid.

14 Ibid.

15 Ibid.

16 Gerald Posner, *Case Closed*, p. 342, WCR, p. 85, HSCA Report, p. 43

17 Jim Moore, *Conspiracy of One*, p. 201

18 Gerald Posner, *Case Closed*, p. 465

19 Ibid. p. 201

20 Ibid. p. 209

21 Ibid. p. 209n

22 Ibid.

23 Priscilla Johnson McMillan, *Marina and Lee*, p. 451

24 WCR, p. 162

25 Gerald Posner, *Case Closed*, p. 213

26 Ibid., p. 214

27 Ibid., p. 215

28 Ibid. pp. 219-220

29 Gaeton Fonzi, *The Last Investigation*, p. 422

30 WCH, vol XXII, p. 613 (CE-1360); vol XVII, p. 3 (CE-769)

31 WCR, p. 31

32 HSCA, vol XI, p. 508

33 WCR, p. 36

34 HSCA, Bruno Deposition, p. 35

35 Ibid. p. 30

36 HSCA, vol XI, p. 515

37 Jim Marrs, *Crossfire*, p. 243

38 HSCA, vol XI, p. 515

39 HSCA, Bruno Deposition, p. 45

40 WCH, vol VII, p. 443

41 WCH, vol XXII, p. 613 (CE-1360)

42 HSCA, vol XI, p. 508

43 WCR, p. 42

44 WCH, vol VII, p. 446; WCR, p. 43

45 WCR, p. 45

46 Ibid., p. 42

47 HSCA, vol XI, p. 526

48 WCR, p. 43

Chapter 6, *Lee's Motive*
1 Gerald Posner, *Case Closed*, p. 220
2 Ibid., p. 221
3 Ibid., p. 18
4 Ibid.
5 Norman Mailer, *Oswald's Tale*, p. 556
6 Hosty, *Assignment: Oswald*, p. 227
7 WCR, p. 110

PART II, *THE MOB SILENCES LEE*
Chapter 7, *Oswald in the Big Easy*
1 Gerald Posner, *Case Closed*, p. 121
2 John H. Davis, *Mafia Kingfish*, p. 147
3 Anthony Summers, *Conspiracy*, p. 295
4 John H. Davis, *Mafia Kingfish*, p. 249
5 Ibid., p. 175
6 Ibid., p. 171
7 Michael Benson, *Who's Who in the JFK Assassination*, p. 134
8 Ibid., pp. 132-138
9 Ibid., p. 168
10 Ibid., p. 179
11 Ibid., p. 168
12 Fred Emery, *Watergate*, p. xviii
13 Robert J. Groden, *The Search for Lee Harvey Oswald*, p. 18; Anthony Summers, *Conspiracy*, p. 304
14 Michael Benson, *Who's Who in the JFK Assassination*, p. 132
15 Bob Callahan, *Who Shot JFK?*, p. 138
16 Sybil Leek and Burt R. Sugar, *The Assassination Chain*, p. 196
17 John H. Davis, *Mafia Kingfish*, p. 405
18 Michael Benson, *Who's Who in the JFK Assassination*, p. 57
19 Ibid.
20 PBS documentary, *Frontline*, Nov. 16, 1996, Carlos Bringuier interview
21 G. Robert Blakey and Richard N. Billings, *Fatal Hour*, p. 192
22 Ibid., p. 202
23 Warren Hinckle and William Turner, *Deadly Secrets*, p. 243
24 John H. Davis, *Mafia Kingfish*, p. 99
25 Bob Callahan, *Who Shot JFK?*, p. 139
26 John H. Davis, *Mafia Kingfish*, p. 220
27 Bob Callahan, *Who Shot JFK?*, p. 89
28 La Fontaine, *Oswald Talked*, p. 54
29 Norman Mailer, *Oswald's Tale*, p. 618
30 James DiEugenio, *Destiny Betrayed*, p. 42
31 La Fontaine, *Oswald Talked*, p. 54
32 Anthony Summers, *Conspiracy*, p. 302
33 G. Robert Blakey and Richard N. Billings, *Fatal Hour*, p. 375
34 Ibid.
35 Ibid.
36 Discussion with John B. Ciravolo, April 3, 1999
37 Norman Mailer, *Oswald's Tale*, p. 618
38 Ibid., p. 619
39 Anthony Summers, *Conspiracy*, pp. 295-296
40 Ibid., p. 296
41 Ibid., p. 300
42 Ibid., p. 293
43 John H. Davis, *Mafia Kingfish*, p. 175; Anthony Summers, *Conspiracy*, p. 300
44 Jim Garrison, *On the Trail of the Assassins*, p. 178; James DiEugenio, *Destiny Betrayed*, p. 144
45 Anthony Summers, *Conspiracy*, p. 292
46 Ibid., p. 300; John H. Davis, *Mafia Kingfish*, p. 175
47 Anthony Summers, *Conspiracy*, p.288
48 Ibid., p. 300; John H. Davis, *Mafia Kingfish*, p. 175
49 John H. Davis, *Mafia Kingfish*, p. 215; Jim Marrs, *Crossfire*, p. 100
50 John H. Davis, *Mafia Kingfish*, pp. 204, 211
51 Anthony Summers, *Conspiracy*, p. 297
52 La Fontaine, *Oswald Talked*, p. 182
53 John H. Davis, *Mafia Kingfish*, p. 175; Anthony Summers, *Conspiracy*, p. 300
54 Anthony Summers, *Conspiracy*, p. 292

55 Ibid., p. 300; John H. Davis, *Mafia Kingfish*, p. 175

56 Bob Callahan, *Who Shot JFK?*, p. 89

57 Gerald Posner, *Case Closed*, p. 141

58 John H. Davis, *Mafia Kingfish*, p. 175; Anthony Summers, *Conspiracy*, p. 300

59 PBS documentry, *Frontline*, Nov 16, 1996, *Who Was Lee Harvey Oswald?*

60 John H. Davis, *Mafia Kingfish*, p. 175

61 Michael Benson, *Who's Who in the JFK Assassination*, p. 132; Anthony Summers, *Conspiracy*, p. 304

62 John H. Davis, *Mafia Kingfish*, pp. 205-206

63 Jim Garrison, *On the Trail of the Assassins*, p. 144

64 Anthony Summers, *Conspiracy*, p. 283

65 John H. Davis, *Mafia Kingfish*, p. 175; Anthony Summers, *Conspiracy*, p. 300

66 Rosemary James and Jack Wardlaw, *Plot or Politics?* p. 49

67 Anthony Summers, *Conspiracy*, p. 338

68 Ibid., pp. 305-307

69 Gerald Posner, *Case Closed*, p. 146

70 HSCA, Report, pp. 142-143.

71 Michael Benson, *Who's Who in the JFK Assassination*, p. 132; Anthony Summers, *Conspiracy*, p. 304; Dick Russell, *The Man Who Knew Too Much*, p. 720

72 La Fontaine, *Oswald Talked*, p. 182

73 Robert Maheu and Richard Hack, *Next to Hughes*, pp. 108-134

74 G. Robert Blakey and Richard N. Billings, *Fatal Hour*, p. 59

75 Ibid., p. 59

76 Ibid., p. 66

77 Ibid., p. 58

78 Ibid.

79 Ronald Goldfarb, *Perfect Villains, Imperfect Heroes*, p. 264

80 G. Robert Blakey and Richard N. Billings, *Fatal Hour*, p. 59

81 Ibid.

82 Robert Maheu & Richard Hack, *Next to Hughes*, p. 121

83 Ronald Goldfarb, *Perfect Villains, Imperfect Heroes*, p. 264

84 Robert Maheu & Richard Hack, *Next to Hughes*, p. 122

85 Ronald Goldfarb, *Perfect Villains, Imperfect Heroes*, p. 267

86 Ibid., p.266

87 Anthony Summers, *Official and Confidential*, p. 298

88 Lester David and Irene David, *Bobby Kennedy*, pp. 182-183

89 Ronald Goldfarb, *Perfect Villains, Imperfect Heroes*, p. 266

Chapter 8, *The Assassin's Fate is Sealed*

1 Anthony Summers, *Conspiracy*, p. 363

2 Norman Mailer, *Oswald's Tale*, p. 556

3 John H. Davis, *Mafia Kingfish*, pp. 198-199

4 Ibid., p. 198

5 Mark North, *Act of Treason*, p. 408

6 Michael Benson, *Who's Who in the JFK Assassination*, p. 79

7 Ibid., p. 400; La Fontaine, *Oswald Talked*, p. 216

8 Michael Benson, *Who's Who in the JFK Assassination*, pp. 400-401

9 La Fontaine, *Oswald Talked*, p. 213

10 Michael Benson, *Who's Who in the JFK Assassination*, pp. 400-401

11 Mark North, *Act of Treason*, p. 305

12 Seth Kantor, *The Ruby Cover-Up*, pp. 43-44

13 G. Robert Blakey and Richard N. Billings, *Fatal Hour*, p. 337

14 Ibid.

15 John H. Davis, *Mafia Kingfish*, p. 449

16 Ibid., p. 158

17 Ibid.

18 G. Robert Blakey and Richard N. Billings, *Fatal Hour*, p. 361

19 La Fontaine, *Oswald Talked*, p. 216

20 John H. Davis, *Mafia Kingfish*, p. 198

21 Ibid., p. 199

Chapter 9, A Chronology

1 John H. Davis, *Mafia Kingfish*, p. 215; Jim Marrs, *Crossfire*, p. 100

2 John H. Davis, *Mafia Kingfish*, p. 215

3 Ibid.

4 WC, vol XXV, pp. 928-931 (CE-2650)

5 John H. Davis, *Mafia Kingfish*, p. 218

6 Anthony Summers, *Conspiracy*, p. 329

7 Gerald Posner, *Case Closed*, p. 135

8 WCR, pp. 615-617

9 John H. Davis, *Mafia Kingfish*, p. 204

10 Michael Benson, *Who's Who in the JFK Assassination*, p. 400

11 Seth Kantor, *The Ruby Cover-Up*, p. 97

12 John H. Davis, *Mafia Kingfish*, p. 205

13 Ibid., p. 211

14 Ibid., p. 205

15 Ibid., pp. 212-213

16 David E. Scheim, *Contract on America*, p. 275; John Davis, *Mafia Kingfish*, p. 213

17 Bob Callahan, *Who Shot JFK?*, p. 126

18 Anthony Summers, *Conspiracy*, p. 472

19 PBS documentary, *Frontline*, November 16, 1996, Gerald Posner commentary

20 John H. Davis, *Mafia Kingfish*, pp. 213-214

21 Ibid., p. 213

22 Ibid., p. 216

23 Ibid., p. 218

24 Ibid., p. 216

25 Ibid., p. 212

Chapter 10, *The Key Facts*

1 John H. Davis, *Mafia Kingfish*, p. 97

2 G. Robert Blakey and Richard N. Billings, *Fatal Hour*, many; John H. Davis, *Mafia Kingfish*, p. 99

3 John H. Davis, *Mafia Kingfish*, p. 99

4. Warren Hinckle and William Turner, *Deadly Secrets*, p. 242

5 Anthony Summers, *Conspiracy*, pp. 293-296; Michael Benson, *Who's Who in the JFK Assassination*, p. 252

6 G. Robert Blakey and Richard N. Billings, *Fatal Hour*, p. 176

7 La Fontaine, *Oswald Talked*, p. 182

8 Michael Benson, *Who's Who in the JFK Assassination*, p. 132; Anthony Summers, *Conspiracy*, p. 304

9 Anthony Summers, *Conspiracy*, p.363

10 John H. Davis, *Mafia Kingfish*, p. 218; Jim Marrs, *Crossfire*, p. 100

11 John H. Davis, *Mafia Kingfish*, p. 204

12 G. Robert Blakey and Richard N. Billings, *Fatal Hour*, p. 337

13 Michael Benson, *Who's Who in the JFK Assassination*, p. 400

14 Gerald Posner, *Case Closed*, p. 377

15 Michael Benson, *Who's Who in the JFK Assassination*, p. 79

16 John H. Davis, *Mafia Kingfish*, p. 213

17 Seth Kantor, *The Ruby Cover-Up*, pp. 121-149

18 John H. Davis, *Mafia Kingfish*, pp. 211-212

19 G. Robert Blakey and Richard N. Billings, *Fatal Hour*, p. 192

20 Ibid. p. 202

21 Anthony Summers, *Conspiracy*, p. 321

22 Dick Russell, *The Man Who Knew Too Much*, p. 719

23 G. Robert Blakey & Richard N. Billings, *Fatal Hour*, p. 182

24 Ibid.

25 Ibid.

26 Anthony Summers, *Conspiracy*, pp. 317-318

27 Peter Dale Scott, *Deep Politics and the Death of JFK*, p. 88

28 John Newman, *Oswald and the CIA*, p. 320

29 Anthony Summers, *Conspiracy*, p. 318

30 Ibid., p. 321

31 Ibid., p. 503

32 John H. Davis, *Mafia Kingfish*, p. 143

33 Ibid., p. 485

34 Ibid., p. 135

35 Ibid.

36 Ibid., pp. 136-137

37 Gerald Posner, *Case Closed*, p. 124

38 Ibid. p. 136

39 Anthony Summers, *Conspiracy*, p. 310

40 Ibid. p. 312

41 John H. Davis, *Mafia Kingfish*, p. 140

Epilogue

1 Anthony Summers, *Conspiracy*, p. 132

2 Ibid., p. 353-361; PBS documentary, *Frontline*, November 16, 1996

3 Harold Weisberg, *Oswald in New Orleans*, p. 188

4 Ibid. pp. 21, 188, 214, 330, 331; WCR, pp. 483-500

5 Sylvia Meagher, *Accessories After the Fact*, p. 326

6 James P. Hosty, Jr., *Assignment: Oswald*, p. 150

7 John H. Davis, *Mafia Kingfish*, p. 260

8 Michael Benson, *Who's Who in the JFK Assassination*, p. 233

9 James P. Hosty Jr., *Assignment: Oswald*, p. 145

10 Ibid., pp.148-149

11 Ibid., p. 101

12 WCR, p. 449

13 Ibid., p. 451

Appendix I

1 Seth Kantor, *The Ruby Cover-Up*, p. 195

2 Bob Callahan, *Who Shot JFK?*, p. 114

3 Michael Benson, *Who's Who in the JFK Assassination*, p. 456

4 John Davis, *Mafia Kingfish*, p. 155

5 Ibid., p. 85

6 Ibid., p. 155

7 Ibid.

8 Bob Callahan, *Who Shot JFK?*, p. 114

9 Ibid.

10 Seth Kantor, *The Ruby Cover-Up*, p. 52

11 Ibid., p. 55

12 John Davis, *Mafia Kingfish*, p. 585

13 Seth Kantor, *The Ruby Cover-Up*, p. 224

14 Ibid.

15 La Fontaine, *Oswald Talked*, p. 213

16 *Book of Facts, J.F.K. Assassination* (CD-ROM), Macmillan Digital US

17 Ibid.

18 Ibid.

Appendix VI

1 Howard Roffman, *Presumed Guilty*, part II-3

2 HSCA, Vol. I, p. 558

3 Howard Roffman, *Presumed Guilty*, part II-3

4 Ibid.

5 HSCA, Vol. I, p. 555

6 Ibid.

7 Howard Roffman, *Presumed Guilty*, part II-3

8 HSCA, Vol. I, p. 559

9 Ibid., p. 560

10 Ibid., p. 558

11 Fred Litwin, *A Conspiracy Too Big?*, Footnote #7 (Joel Grant's unpublished research paper, *Innuendo Versus Science*)

12 HSCA, Vol. I, p. 560

Index

Note: Page references in italics indicate illustrations.

Failure Analysis Associates (FaAA), 14-16, 23, 165-69

Fair Play for Cuba Committee, 44, 73, 74, 75, 80, 115

Falter, Dr. Esmond, 80

FBI (Federal Bureau of Investigation)
Banister and, 73, 74, 105*n*, 114
Bogard and, 54
Brand and, 55
CIA-Mafia debacle and, 83*n*-85*n*
Dallas Police Department and, 114
De Laparra and, 107*n*
Ferrie and, 95, 101, 102, 104, 105, 112, 113-14
JFK and, ix, 114
Lake Pontchartrain training camp raid by, 77, 106*n*, 107*n*
Maheu and, 82
Marcello and, 77, 88, *90*
Moore and, 90*n*
neutron activation analysis by, *16*, 17, 17*n*, 18*n*, 19-20, 42*n*, 62, 172-75
O'Sullivan and, 78
Oswald and, 52, 57, 66, 101, 105*n*, 115
on rifle, 27
Shaw and, 114
and SOLO, 67
spectographic testing by, 19-20, 21*n*, 37, 38, 171-72
Warren Commission and, 13, 113-14

Felix Oyster House, 107*n*

Fenner, Nanny, 57

Ferrie, David, *90*
Banister and, 74-76, 78, 79, 80, 81
Castro and, 74-75, 76
CIA and, 75, 82, 88, 93, 109*n*
in Civil Air Patrol, 75-76, 77, 79, 80-82, 103
Dallas, en route to, 80, 91, 94, 96, 104, 111-12, 113-14
FBI and, 95, 101, 102, 104, 105, 112, 113-14
in Galveston, 96, *96*, 100, *101*, 104
in Houston, 94, 95, 96, *96*, 102, 105, 112
JFK and, 74-75, 87-88
and library card story, 93, 93*n*-94*n*, 95-96, 100-102, *101*, 104

Mafia and, 74, 88, 93
Marcello and, 74, 75, 77, 87-89, *90*, 93, 97, 107*n*, 111-12
in New Orleans, 74-76, 77-83, 87-88, 91, 102
Oswald and, 67, 75-76, 76*n*, 77-83, 79, 88, 91, 93-97, 100-105, 107*n*, 109*n*, 113

Film, Zapruder, 6, 15, 16, 18, 20, 21-22

Finck, Dr. Pierre, 17

Fitzgerald, Desmond, 109*n*

Ford, Gerald, 14

Fort Worth, 61

Frazier, Buell Wesley, 30, 41, 54, 66

Frazier, Robert, 16-17, 18*n*, *19*

Fritz, John W., 114

Frontline, 14

Galveston, Texas, 96, *96*, 100, *101*, 104

Gambling, 107*n*-108*n*

Garner, Jesse, 93, 93*n*-94*n*, 95, 100-101, *101*

Garrison, Jim, 75

Gaudet, William, 81

Giancana, Sam, 82, 83*n*-84*n*, 85*n*, 88, *90* , 103

Gill, Wray, 74, 95, 100, *101*

Givens, Charles, 26

Grant, Eva, 90*n*

Greer, William, *19*

Gregory, Dr., 13

Groden, Robert J., 123

Guatemala, 74, 77

Guinn, Dr. Vincent, 17, 17*n*, 18*n*, 19-20, 42*n*, 173-75

Gunman, gunmen, 5-7, 11, 20-21, 23, 25, 42*n*, 62

Hands Off Cuba, 73, 75

Hard Copy, 62

Hardy's shoe store, 37